SANTA ANNA

MILITARY PROFILES

SERIES EDITOR

Dennis E. Showalter, Ph.D.
Colorado College

*Instructive summaries for general and expert
readers alike, volumes in the Military Profiles
series are essential treatments of significant and
popular military figures drawn from world history,
ancient times through the present.*

AVAILABLE IN 2002

SANTA ANNA

A Curse upon Mexico

Robert L. Scheina

Brassey's, Inc.
Washington, D.C.

Library of Congress Cataloging-in-Publication Data
Scheina, Robert L.
Santa Anna : a curse upon Mexico /
Robert L. Scheina. — 1st ed.
p. cm.
Includes bibliographical references and index.
ISBN 1-57488-405-0 (alk. paper)
1. Santa Anna, Antonio López de, 1794?–1876.
2. Mexico — History — 1821–1861. I. Title.
F1232.S232 S34 2002
972'.04'092 — dc21   2002002481

Printed in the United States of America on acid-free paper that meets the American National Standards Institute z39-48 Standard.

Brassey's, Inc.
22841 Quicksilver Drive
Dulles, Virginia 20166

FIRST EDITION

10 9 8 7 6 5 4 3 2 1

Contents

Maps

Preface

Antonio López de Santa Anna was a soldier. But like so many Latin American soldiers who won the presidency through success on the battlefield, he has been more frequently judged by his political decisions than his military ones. For the most part, these political decisions were catastrophic for Mexico, and earned Santa Anna a black image.

To accurately judge Santa Anna, we must evaluate him within his political, social, and economic context. When placed within this context, we see Santa Anna in a different light. Although he is perhaps no more likable, his skills, which permitted him to thrive within that environment, are more apparent.

Santa Anna was a soldier in a feudal-like world. *Criollos* (Mexicans claiming pure Spanish blood) were the knights, rooks, and bishops in this real-life game of chess; the poor were the pawns. And one of these *criollos* would scramble to the top of the mountain and declare himself president. How long he remained at the top depended upon his ability to manipulate his competitors. Remarkably, Antonio López de Santa Anna excelled at this game — he became president eleven times!

As a soldier, Santa Anna is remembered mostly for his defeats at San Jacinto, Buena Vista, Cerro Gordo, and elsewhere at the hands of "gringo" generals who led highly motivated, citizen armies. But in his own feudal-like realm, Santa Anna was bold, brave, and victorious. These attributes are the ones that earn him a place in this series dedicated to military leaders.

I could not write a book related to the history of Mexico without the help of the following good friends and scholars. First and foremost is my mentor, Dr. Richard Greenleaf, who for almost forty years has provided boundless encouragement. Next I must thank Dr. Barbara Tenenbaum, the Mexican Specialist at the Hispanic-American Division, Library of Congress, for always knowing where to find the answer and unselfishly helping. Third, I am indebted to my classmate of forty years, *Licenciado* Nancy Gurrola of the Universidad Iberoamericana, Mexico City, for providing hard-to-come-by items. Fourth, I need to thank Dr. James Riley of the Catholic University, Washington, DC, for his continual support. And I want to thank Mr. John Klingemann of Sul Ross University, Texas, for sharing his unique insights.

Finally, this work would not have been written without the help, sacrifices, and encouragement of Linda, my wife, or the opportunity provided by my agent, Fritz Heinzen.

The views expressed in this book are those of the author and do not reflect the official policy or position of the National Defense University, the Department of Defense, or the U.S. Government.

Chronology

	Valentín Gómez Farías and retired to his ranch
1834, April 24	Fourth presidency—returned to Mexico City and seized the presidency (technically, from himself)
1835, January 28	Temporarily relinquished presidency to Miguel Barragan to campaign in Texas
1836, March 6	Victorious at the Battle of the Alamo in San Antonio, Texas
1836, April 21	Defeated and captured at the Battle of San Jacinto, Texas
1837, February 21	Landed at Vera Cruz, returning from captivity
1838, December 5	Lost lower left leg while attacking a retiring French landing party at Vera Cruz
1839, March 18	Fifth presidency—Congress chose Santa Anna as interim president to replace Carlos Bustamante
1839, April 30	Victorious at Puebla
1839, July 10	Relinquished presidency back to Carlos Bustamante because of "poor health"
1841, October 10	Sixth presidency of Santa Anna
1842, October 26	Temporarily relinquished presidency to Nicolás Bravo and retired to his ranch
1843, March 5	Seventh presidency—returned to Mexico City and reclaimed office
1843, October 4	Temporarily relinquished presidency to Valentín Canalizo and retired to his ranch
1844, June 4	Eighth presidency—returned to Mexico City and reclaimed office
1844, August 23	Wife, Doña Inés, died at age of 33
1844, September 12	Temporarily relinquished presidency to José Joaquín de Herrera and retired to his ranch
1844, October 3	Married 15-year-old María Dolores Tosta
1845, June	Exiled to Venezuela but stopped and remained in Cuba

1846, September 15	Entered Mexico City after being permitted through the American blockade
1846, December 24	Elected provisional president (but since the constitution prohibited an individual from commanding the army in the field and being president at the same time, Santa Anna is not considered to have been officially president)
1847, February 23	Withdrew from the Battle of Buena Vista
1847, March 21	Ninth presidency of Santa Anna
1847, April 2	Temporarily relinquished presidency to Pedro María Anaya and retired to his ranch
1847, April 18	Defeated at Battle of Cerro Gordo
1847, May 20	Tenth presidency of Santa Anna
1847, September 16	Relinquished presidency to a triumvirate
1847, October 7	Ordered to relinquish command of the army
1848, April 5	Exiled to Jamaica, but moved to Nueva Granada (the future Colombia)
1853, April 1	Landed in Vera Cruz after Conservatives called him back
1853, April 20	Eleventh presidency of Santa Anna
1853, December 16	Declared dictator for one year
1854, December 1	Manipulated a favorable plebiscite for continuance of dictatorship
1855, August 9	Exiled first to Cuba, then Colombia, and finally St. Thomas
1864, February 28	Landed at Vera Cruz after promising not to participate in politics
1866, March 12	Exiled from Mexico following the issuing of a public statement under his signature
1866, May 12	Landed in New York
1867, June 7	Unsuccessfully attempted to land at Vera Cruz
1867, June 12	Arrested at Sisal, Yucatán

1867, November 1	Sailed from Vera Cruz to exile in Cuba, then Puerto Plata, and finally Nassau
1874, February 27	Permitted to return to Mexico and landed at Vera Cruz
1874, March 7	Returned to Mexico City
1876, June 21	Died; was buried the following day

SANTA ANNA

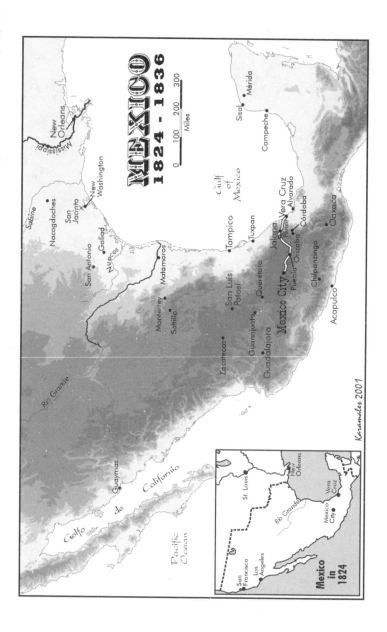

MEXICO
1824 - 1836

0   100   200   300
Miles

New Orleans
Mississippi
New Washington
San Jacinto
Sabine
Nacogdoches
San Antonio
Goliad
Nueces
Matamoros
Monterrey
Saltillo
San Luis Potosi
Queretaro
Tampico
Tuxpan
Gulf of Mexico
Sisal
Mérida
Campeche
Vera Cruz
Alvarado
Perote
Jalapa
Cordoba
Orizaba
Puebla
Mexico City
Chilpanzingo
Oaxaca
Acapulco
Guanajuato
Guadalajara
Zacatecas
Rio Grande
Guaymas
Golfo de California
Pacific Ocean

Karamelas 2001

Mexico in 1824

St. Louis
New Orleans
San Francisco
Los Angeles
Rio Grande
Vera Cruz
Mexico City

Mexico
in 1824

Chapter 1

The Road to "Revolution"

F EW INDIVIDUALS have caused their nation greater pain than Antonio López de Santa Anna. He lost one third of Mexico's territory in wars (918,345 square miles). He sold another 29,670 square miles (the Gadsden Purchase) and pocketed much of the money. He not only bankrupted the nation but also made it heavily indebted to foreigners by agreeing to usurious interest rates. His legendary extravagance was exemplified by the burial of his amputated leg at great expense to Mexico. He made a mockery of the political system during his eleven terms as president — even overthrowing himself (an *auto-golpe*) on one occasion. He stole, forged documents, gambled excessively, womanized, on occasion used narcotics, and increasingly became an egocentric braggart.[1]

How could such a devious individual rise above all others to determine the fate of Mexico for almost thirty years? The answer lies not just in the man but also in his times.

The Mexico of 1810 had changed little in 300 years. Spain had conquered the Aztec Empire in 1521 and expanded into adjacent regions that collectively became known as New Spain, the future

Mexico. The new colony possessed large amounts of gold and silver but also a large Indian population—perhaps 30 million inhabitants. Spain's challenge was how to subjugate so many while exploiting so much. The solution lay in social, economic, and political controls.

Socially, Spain created a strict racial hierarchy that placed those born in Spain (known as *gachupines*) at the top of the pyramid; those born in the New World of pure Spanish descent (known as *criollos*) were next; those of mixed European and Indian blood (known as *mestizos*) followed the *criollos;* near the bottom of the pyramid were the pure-blooded Indians; and, ultimately, the lowest of the low, were the black slaves. One of the teachings of the Catholic Church that complemented the king's social goals was that an individual would be rewarded for a righteous life—which included loyalty to the king—in the hereafter and not necessarily in the here and now. Therefore, to be a good Christian, one needed to be a good subject and content with his or her social status.

Spain's economic philosophy of mercantilism reinforced this racial hierarchy. Mercantilism required that colonies exist for the good of the mother country. This meant that colonial goods could not compete with those of Spain or any other Spanish colony to which the motherland wished to grant special favor. Also, the king frequently sold trade monopolies for financial or political reasons. Most frequently, these went to *gachupines.*

Politically, the king granted the highest offices in the New World to *gachupines.* In 1808, of the ninety-nine individuals serving in the *audiencias* (colonial governments), only twenty-five were *criollos;* the remainder were *gachupines.*

Gachupine generals also controlled the military, but most of the lesser officers were *criollos.* The Royalist Army of Mexico in 1810 numbered 33,000 men, mostly militia. However, the system was so corrupt that many of these troops probably existed only on paper so that their officers could pocket the monies sent to support them. The army had a disproportionately high number of officers—perhaps half the total—because the king frequently sold military commissions to raise money. And there were good reasons to buy a commission. For instance, the military had a separate court system known as the *fuero*. It had jurisdiction over all civil and criminal cases involving those in the military. In practical terms, this system placed those in the army above civilian law.[2]

Many common soldiers were debtors who chose the army over prison. When the need became great, impressment gangs roamed the countryside and forced peasants into the army. The Spanish colonial army perceived two threats — marauding, savage Indians in northern old Mexico, and seaborne raids by Spain's European enemies. Unexpectedly in 1810, Father Miguel Hidalgo began a revolution that rapidly took on the dimensions of a class struggle — the "haves" (most of the *gachupines* and many *criollos*) against the "have-nots" (a few liberal *criollos,* and many *mestizos,* Indians, and blacks).

Such was the world of Antonio López de Santa Anna, a *criollo* born in 1794. His position in society was toward the top of the social pyramid, but he had limitations. His family possessed only modest wealth, and he was a *veracruzano* (from the province of Vera Cruz) and not from the capital. The prejudices of that day held that birth in a tropical environment like Vera Cruz weakened European blood.[3]

His birthplace, the city of Jalapa, did hold strategic importance. Jalapa lay on the Royal Road (soon to be renamed the National Road) between Mexico City, which was 250 miles to the west, and the port of Vera Cruz, 35 miles to the southeast. Mexico City was the political heart of Mexico; Vera Cruz, through the customs house, was the source of the government's revenues. Whoever controlled movement between the capital and Vera Cruz held the purse strings of Mexico. This control could most safely be exerted from some location above the coastal plain, which from mid-May through mid-September was plagued by the "Black Vomit" (yellow fever). Jalapa, which lay directly above the unhealthy lowlands, was just such a location.

Antonio's father encouraged him to seek a career in commerce, but the spirited boy preferred the army. He was ambitious, handsome, and tall — 5 feet 10 inches in a society where the norm was 5 feet 6 — which were natural assets for a military career. Soon after his decision to enter the army, Antonio began modeling his appearance on Napoleon Bonaparte, even though the Frenchman was despised in Mexico for his invasion of Spain: he combed his hair back to front, and he exhibited a preference for riding white horses.[4]

On 9 June 1810, Antonio López de Santa Anna was commissioned a "gentleman cadet" *(caballero cadete),* a title reserved for those from distinguished families, into the Permanent *[Fijo]* Infantry Regiment of Vera Cruz. As a young cadet, he campaigned in the provinces of Nuevo Santander (today's Tamaulipas) and Texas. Briefly, he served in a cavalry unit commanded by the future emperor of Mexico, *criollo* Agustín de Iturbide, during which time Santa Anna was wounded in the left shoulder by an Indian arrow. On 18 August 1813, Santa Anna fought against revolutionaries at Medina, Texas, and won a badge *(escudo)* for courage. The enemy included many North American adventurers who, although brave, were undisciplined. This was probably Santa Anna's first battle against "gringos," and the poor performance of these freebooters probably left the impression that the North Americans did not make good soldiers.[5]

At this time a character flaw emerged, one that would surface again and again. Santa Anna was caught forging the signatures of senior officers to draw on his company's funds and pay off gambling debts. The regimental surgeon advanced Santa Anna 300 pesos to repay the money, but practically everything Santa Anna owned, including his saber, was confiscated to help pay the debt. This scandal would resurface from time to time as Santa Anna's career came increasingly into the public arena.[6]

In 1814 Santa Anna transferred to the Second Battalion of Grenadiers stationed in the port of Vera Cruz. Tactics had changed significantly since the early days of the Hidalgo rebellion. By 1815 the most prominent revolutionary leaders — Fathers Miguel Hidalgo and José Morelos — had been captured and executed. No large revolutionary forces remained in the field, and the war had evolved into one in which the royalists occupied the major cities and towns and the revolutionaries roamed the countryside, attacking commercial and private travelers as they passed between the royalist strongholds. Adapting to this new threat, Viceroy Félix Calleja, an accomplished soldier, organized "flying detachments" *(estacamentos volantes)*. These mounted troops sought out and destroyed the rebels, punished those suspected of aiding the revolution, and convoyed travelers between the major cities. Santa Anna served in these fast-moving, instant dispensers of royal justice. In 1815 he fought in Cotaxtla and Sancampuz and helped capture Boquilla de Piedra, all towns in the Province of Vera Cruz; for this he was awarded a second badge for bravery.

By 1821 the royalist strategy in Mexico had been largely successful. Mexican royalists had hunted down most of the revolutionary leaders. The only prominent fugitives were Guadelupe Victoria, who was hiding in a cave, and the guerrilla warrior Vicente Guerrero, who was protected by the ruggedness of the southern mountains. However, the Mexican royalists could not influence events in Spain, events that jeopardized their colonial status: The Liberals forced the recalcitrant King Ferdinand VII to accept a liberal constitution. The Mexican royalists had no desire to be governed by a liberal constitution that would limit or even eliminate many of their privileges.[7]

On 24 February 1821, the *criollo* royalist Agustín de Iturbide declared the "Plan of Iguala" and made a deal with the revolutionary Vicente Guerrero. The plan called for (1) Mexico to be independent under a constitutional monarchy, preferably chosen from the Bourbon dynasty; (2) the church to retain its privileges; and (3) all distinctions of race to be abolished.

While these events were playing out, Santa Anna, now a royalist captain, was given command of the Permanent Lancers of Vera Cruz in March 1821. Early in the morning of the 29th, he defeated the wily old revolutionary José Miranda at Orizaba (for which the Spanish Viceroy promoted him to lieutenant colonel). In spite of his victory, a large body of revolutionaries, commanded by Colonel José Joaquín Herrera, closed in on Santa Anna from all sides. If this predicament and Herrera's presence were not enough incentives to change sides, Santa Anna had another—he had never repaid the surgeon the 300 pesos to cover his forgeries. At two o'clock the same afternoon, Antonio López de Santa Anna declared his support for the revolutionary Plan of Iguala, thereby changing sides and garnishing for himself yet another promotion, now to colonel in the revolutionary forces.[8]

Santa Anna's defection was a serious loss for the royalists because he was their most effective field commander along the critical route between Vera Cruz and Jalapa. Some 600 infantrymen followed Santa Anna to the revolutionary side. They marched on the royalist stronghold at the port of Alvarado about forty-five miles southeast of the port of Vera Cruz where the royalists surrendered without a fight. Santa Anna then rescued revolutionary forces besieged in Córdoba, some sixty miles northwest of Jalapa on the National Road. Not a modest man, Santa Anna described the battle in these words: "Very opportune was my arrival in Córdoba; only one wall remained for the defense of the patriots. The conflict was severe and the exigencies in proportion. It was necessary to take the offensive quickly and actively, and I took it at all risk with two thousand men and six cannon. Fortune favored my efforts. . . ."[9]

Santa Anna next captured Jalapa, his birthplace, and then captured the fortifications protecting the Puente del Rey (Bridge of the King) spanning the Antigua River.[10]

Santa Anna now marched on Vera Cruz, the fortifications of which had received special attention from Spain throughout the colonial period. Santa Anna attacked the city on 7 July 1821, but the revolutionaries broke and ran when confronted by Spanish regulars. Santa Anna, supported by a handful of men, covered the flight and was among the last of the revolutionaries to leave the battlefield. He withdrew to the high ground of Córdoba and Jalapa.[11]

Santa Anna traveled to Puebla, eighty miles east of Mexico City, to confer with the recently self-proclaimed leader of the revolution, Agustín de Iturbide. Together, they decided that Vera Cruz should be ignored for a few months to avoid the yellow fever season and instead Santa Anna should attack Fortress Perote. Although the old fortress was only twenty miles west of Jalapa, by road it was a forty-mile journey because of hilly terrain; the National Road rose there to an altitude of 4,000 feet.

On 30 July 1821, the representative of the new Liberal government in Spain, Lieutenant General Juan O'Donoju, arrived at Vera Cruz. This new viceroy found the port under light attack by Santa Anna's forces. Santa Anna facilitated a meeting between O'Donoju and Iturbide. On 24 August, the two men signed the Treaty of Córdoba whereby the viceroy accepted the Plan of Iguala in the name of Spain. Under this treaty, should a prince of the House of Bourbon not accept the Mexican crown, an assembly of Mexicans would then choose a countryman as sovereign.

Santa Anna's attention remained focused on capturing Perote. It surrendered on 7 October following a twenty-six-day siege. Also at this time, Mexico City surrendered to Iturbide. Santa Anna now marched against Vera Cruz. Spanish General José Dávila realized that he could not continue to defend Vera Cruz against the growing power of the revolutionaries. He retreated into the Fortress San Juan de Ulúa, situated on a tiny island inside the harbor; from there the fortress's commander could significantly disrupt the port's commerce. The leading citizens of Vera Cruz feared Santa Anna and petitioned Iturbide to allow some other revolutionary to accept the surrender of the city. Iturbide ordered Colonel Manuel Rincón to accept the surrender, which he did when he, along with Santa Anna, entered the port on 27 October. Iturbide appointed Rincón governor and ordered Santa Anna to leave the city for a well-deserved rest.[12]

To the surprise of only the most naive, neo-revolutionary Agustín de Iturbide crowned himself Agustín I, Emperor of Mexico, on 19 May 1822, and received a letter of unqualified allegiance from now–Brigadier General Antonio López de Santa Anna. He wrote, "In common with the regiment of the line number 8 which I command, and which under my direction was ready to take such a politic and glorious step [of acclaiming you emperor] much soon[er] than the present time, I regret that we were not the instruments of such a worthy recognition."[13]

The coronation of Iturbide was in reality a victory for the Conservatives (formerly royalists) over the Liberals (formerly old-line revolutionaries). The degree of subordination of the Liberals to the Conservatives may be measured by the military posts assigned and promotions given to members from each political persuasion following the creation of the new Mexican Empire. Mexico was divided into five military zones *(capitanías generales)*. Only one of these, the poorest region, was commanded by an old-line revolutionary. Four of the five new marshals were former royalists. The only lieutenant general and the minister of war and marine were both Spaniards who professed allegiance to Mexico. Eight of the nine new brigadiers were former royalists.[14]

Like the Spanish king before him, Emperor Agustín I found selling military commissions an expedient method to raise money and reward followers. The new Mexican army in the capital was composed of 8,308 soldiers; 3,161 sergeants, corporals, and musicians; and 1,802 officers. The emperor also created the "Order of Guadalupe" which possessed degrees of eminence. Santa Anna received the Order of Guadalupe, "cruz de número" (numbered cross), which was a second-degree order. And finally, on 25 September, Iturbide appointed Santa Anna the military commander of Vera Cruz.[15]

Antonio López de Santa Anna should have been pleased with his choice of careers. To rise from cadet to brigadier in fewer than twelve years was rapid advancement in any man's army. But Iturbide had jumped other officers two and three grades and, to Santa Anna's mind, surely they were less deserving. Santa Anna was frustrated, undoubtedly believing that he was inadequately rewarded for having "made" the Mexican Empire possible by becoming a revolutionary at a critical moment.[16]

Chapter 2

The Road to Becoming a *Caudillo*

W HILE EMPEROR AGUSTÍN I was attempting to consolidate his political position, Brigadier General Santa Anna was scheming to win national recognition. In October 1822, Santa Anna conspired with Spanish Brigadier Francisco Lemaur, who now commanded the Spanish garrison in Fortress San Juan de Ulúa. Santa Anna would permit Lemaur to recapture the port of Vera Cruz without a fight in exchange for an appropriate reward. In reality, this was a ruse on the part of Santa Anna; he planned to trap the Spaniards. Santa Anna's immediate superior, General José Antonio Echávarri—the Captain General of the provinces of Puebla, Vera Cruz, and Oaxaca—had approved the scheme and was to take part in the capture.[1]

Santa Anna asked Echávarri to position himself at the *Concepcion* redoubt near the gate by the same name where Echávarri was to command a large force. When Echávarri arrived, he found himself almost alone. Suddenly a large Spanish force landed, and Echávarri had barely enough time to call a Mexican cavalry squadron to his rescue. At all the other gates, Santa Anna had positioned large forces, and they captured some 300 Spaniards. The remaining Spaniards recognized the trap and retreated back to Fortress San Juan de Ulúa. Santa Anna claimed a victory while Echávarri wrote to Iturbide accusing Santa Anna of trying to cause his capture or death out of jealousy.[2]

Iturbide was well aware of Santa Anna's boundless ambition — Santa Anna had attempted to court Iturbide's sister, who was more than thirty years Santa Anna's senior. Iturbide, heading a small force, marched from Mexico City to Jalapa, ostensibly to evaluate the Spanish defenses in Fortress San Juan de Ulúa but in reality to deal with Santa Anna. Calling the maverick general to the provincial capital, the emperor removed Santa Anna as the commander of Vera Cruz and ordered him to report to Mexico City. Santa Anna had little choice but to agree to go to the capital. Before leaving, he requested and received permission to return to Vera Cruz in order to put his affairs in order. In typically flamboyant language, Santa Anna described his feelings, "So rude a blow wounded my military pride and tore the bandage from my eyes. I beheld absolutism in all its power; and I felt encouraged to enter into a struggle against Agustín Iturbide. . . ."[3] At about the same time, the old revolutionary Guadalupe Victoria contacted Santa Anna, and together they conspired to overthrow Iturbide and to establish a republic.[4]

In Vera Cruz, Santa Anna proclaimed the Republic of Mexico on 6 December 1822. Surprisingly, Santa Anna accepted support from Brigadier Lemaur, the commander of Spanish forces in San Juan de Ulúa. Santa Anna marched toward Jalapa. South of the provincial capital at Plan del Río, he captured a detachment of Imperial Grenadiers (elite troops), most of whom switched sides and joined Santa Anna. On the 21st Santa Anna, leading 400 men, attempted to storm Jalapa. The grenadiers deserted and a significant number of Santa Anna's men were trapped and forced to surrender. Seeing his force decimated, Santa Anna panicked and fled. As he passed over the Puente del Rey, he encountered Guadalupe Victoria. Santa Anna suggested that they flee to the

United States; Guadalupe Victoria counseled instead that Santa Anna fortify the port of Vera Cruz while he rallied support throughout the countryside.[5]

Santa Anna and his followers retreated into the walled port of Vera Cruz. To deal with the rebellious Santa Anna, Iturbide sent General Echávarri at the head of 3,000 troops. Echávarri should have taken great pleasure in getting even with Santa Anna. A long siege seemed inevitable since Echávarri commanded mostly cavalry and light field artillery, both ill suited to capturing a walled city. Unexpectedly, on 1 February Echávarri and thirty-three of his officers proclaimed the "Plan of Casa Mata." This plan and the one proclaimed by Santa Anna earlier merged into one anti-Iturbide movement.[6]

By 19 February 1823, Iturbide appreciated the rising tide against him and abdicated his throne. The empire ceased to exist. While individuals of national prominence, which included many military officers senior to Santa Anna, debated the future of the nation in Mexico City, Santa Anna began a new military campaign against an invisible enemy. Taking 500 infantry and 50 cavalry he embarked at Vera Cruz and sailed 240 miles north-northwest to Tampico, landing on 1 April. He immediately marched inland to San Luís Potosí. On his own authority, he seized a silver bar from the local treasury and had it minted into coins to pay expenses.

While in San Luís Potosí, Santa Anna attended cockfights by day and gambled by night, maintaining poor discipline over his troops. His infantry's and cavalry's quarrels often came to blows; half a dozen were killed during one brawl.

On 5 June Santa Anna proclaimed a federal republic, which gave the states significant political power. (Meanwhile, the senior statesmen in Mexico City were doing the same — the Liberals also announced the creation of a federal republic. They preferred a defusion of power to the states, unlike the Conservatives, who wanted the power to reside in Mexico City.)

However, the Twelfth Regiment, which was garrisoned in San Luís Potosí, opposed a federal government and was supported by the town's leading citizens. This regiment seized strategic sites throughout the town and prepared to fight Santa Anna's troops. But because the regiment lacked a strong leader, these soldiers gradually abandoned their positions.

When Mexico City learned of the unrest in San Luís Potosí, Generals Pedro Negrete and Nicolás Bravo led government troops toward the city from the capital. Santa Anna withdrew from the San Luís Potosí and on 10 July professed his loyalty to the new national government. He was subjected to a court martial for having fomented unrest. The court acquitted him, finding it impossible to find Santa Anna guilty of declaring a federal republic while those in Mexico City were doing the same.[7]

Guadalupe Victoria became the first president of Mexico on 10 October 1824 under the new Constitution of 1824, at least in some measure, thanks to Antonio López de Santa Anna. The new president "rewarded" Santa Anna by sending him to the Yucatán to resolve a long-standing commercial dispute between the ports of Mérida and Campeche. Mérida traded primarily with Havana and secretly wanted either to remain within the Spanish Empire, with which Mexico was still at war, or become the capital of an independent Yucatán. Campeche supported an independent Mexico. To Santa Anna, the "reward" seemed hardly commensurate with the service he had rendered. Not coincidentally, this task also removed Santa Anna from the mainstream of Mexican political life. Just before leaving for the Yucatán, Santa Anna (then 31 years old) married Doña Inés García, a fourteen-year-old *gachupina,* who brought a moderate dowry.

While dealing with the problem in the Yucatán, Santa Anna proposed to Mexico City a plan to invade Spanish-held Cuba and began working on the details. Senior officials in the capital perceived this scheme as a possible solution to the "Santa Anna problem." The Mexican Foreign Minister, Manuel Gómez Pedraza, observed, "If it succeeds it ought to be a great honor to Mexico; if it fails at least it will rid us of Santa Anna."[8]

Mexico City chose to ignore Santa Anna's planning but not so the United States. It had its own designs on Cuba. In order to assuage the concerns of the United States, the Mexican government recalled Santa Anna from the Yucatán to Mexico City. Much to his credit, Santa Anna had temporarily ended the squabbling between Mérida and Campeche before his recall.[9]

These were tough economic times for Mexico. The new federal republic was plagued by greedy men who swarmed about the treasury like locusts, and by the Spaniards, who controlled the harbor of Vera Cruz from Fortress San Juan de Ulúa and squeezed the commercial life out of the port. On 30 December 1825, Mexico's first vice president, Conservative Nicolás Bravo, rebelled against Liberal President Guadalupe Victoria. Before the rebellion gained headway, General Vicente Guerrero quickly moved to crush it. Then Santa Anna wrote to President Victoria condemning the rebellion and offering his services to what would obviously be the winning side. The rebellion almost immediately collapsed. In spite of the fact that Santa Anna had taken no military action, many perceived him as a successful defender of the president.[10]

Miraculously, Guadalupe Victoria served out his full four-year term (1824–29), the only Mexican president to do so until the 1860s. Guadalupe Victoria was also one of the few Mexican presidents to leave office as poor as when he entered. The continuing animosity between the Liberals and Conservatives guaranteed that the selection of Victoria's successor would be contentious at best. Such a political environment was fertile ground for exploitation by Antonio López de Santa Anna.

The 1829 presidential contest was between Liberal Vicente Guerrero and Conservative Manuel Gómez Pedraza. Guerrero, an uneducated *mestizo* from the poor south, was an old-line revolutionary. Pedraza, a *criollo* scholar, had been foreign minister and minister of war in the Victoria government. Pedraza won the election by gaining the votes of ten of the nineteen state legislatures as required by law, but Guerrero was the more popular with the people. The Liberals charged that Pedraza had used the army to intimidate the state legislators.[11]

On 11 September, Santa Anna rode west along the National

Road. With bravado and a few followers, he seized Fortress Perote. On 16 September, the eighteenth anniversary of Mexico's "Call to Independence" by Father Miguel Hidalgo, Santa Anna declared against Gómez Pedraza. "How could I see in cold blood the republic converted into a vast Inquisition? Santa Anna will die before being indifferent to such disasters."[12]

However, Santa Anna had acted prematurely and was not immediately joined by pro-Guerrero followers as he had expected. He learned that overwhelming government forces commanded by General José María Calderón were approaching. Calderón was known to be a very cautious man; so Santa Anna, leading 625 men, retreated southward across the mountains to Oaxaca, which he seized. Staying ahead of the Conservative Calderón was an easy matter for Santa Anna.[13]

Typical of the impulsive acts for which Santa Anna was now known, he dressed some of his men as priests, and on 29 November they unsuccessfully tried to capture General Calderón at Mass on 29 November. Calderón fortunately had chosen to attend Mass elsewhere. (Lest the effort be entirely in vain, Santa Anna's men made off with the collection.) Calderón besieged Santa Anna at Oaxaca; and on 30 November, just when it appeared that Santa Anna must surrender, an army unit near Mexico City joined the rebellion. Then key political figures Lorenzo de Zavala and Vicente Guerrero also rebelled against Gómez Pedraza. Three days later, disgusted with the turn of events, Gómez Pedraza quit the fight.[14]

Responding to a letter from Guerrero thanking him for his support, Santa Anna wrote: "My beloved friend and companion: What thing can be asked of me in the name of my country and by my worthy friend, the patriot Vicente Guerrero, that I will not do?"[15]

In order to pacify the yet undefeated Conservatives, the Liberals permitted Conservative Anastasio Bustamante to be chosen Guerrero's vice president. As a reward for his services, Santa Anna was promoted to general of division, the highest rank in the army. He could now claim with some accuracy to have caused the downfall of an emperor (Iturbide) and the selection of a president (Guerrero).[16]

Santa Anna triumphantly returned to Jalapa but now at the head of 1,000 men — far more than those with which he left. He asked the town fathers for voluntary contributions to maintain his new following. When they reported that not enough money had been contributed to maintain all, Santa Anna asked for the names of those who had not given. Soon, the money flowed in.[17]

By 1828 Antonio López de Santa Anna had become a full-fledged caudillo. Derived from the Latin *capitellum* meaning "a small head," a *caudillo* was an individual who placed himself above the law and commanded a significant following because of his success on the battlefield and his ability to reward his followers. No matter what it might take — forced loans, outright theft, or even the sale of the national territory — money was as much a key to success for a *caudillo* as was *bravado*.[18]

A measure of a caudillo's power was his land holdings. During the 1820s, Santa Anna acquired his ranch *(finca) Manga de Clavo* (Clove Spike). As Santa Anna's political power grew, so did his ranch, and at the expense of his neighbors. It ultimately stretched almost from the city of Jalapa to the port of Vera Cruz, a distance of thirty-five miles. By 1845 the ranch would encompass 483,000 acres of land and support 40,000 head of cattle and thousands of horses.[19]

Chapter 3

The Road to Tampico

In 1829, neither Spain nor Mexico believed that the war for Mexican independence was over. Many *gachupines* and conservative *criollos* in Mexico urged the Spanish king to send a military expedition, around which they could rally and restore Mexico as a colony. Spain had been attentively watching the endless factionalism in Mexico and believed the time was now right to reconquer the rebellious colony. On 6 July 1829, a large but poorly outfitted Spanish invasion force sailed from Cuba. Rear Admiral Ángel Laborde commanded one ship-of-the-line, two frigates, two smaller warships, and fifteen transports carrying some 3,000 men. On 16 July, 2,600 Spanish troops commanded by Brigadier Isidro Barradas landed at Cabo Rojo, about sixty miles south of Tampico (400 had been shipwrecked off the Louisiana coast in a heavy storm). The fleet immediately returned to Cuba. As the troops marched into Tampico on 6 August, they did not receive the warm welcome from the populace they had expected. The situation immediately worsened as yellow fever broke out.[1]

Santa Anna, now governor of the state of Vera Cruz, had been preparing for the long-expected invasion. Once he learned that the Spaniards had landed near Tampico, he gathered 2,000 troops (half of whom were militia) and supplies and extracted a 20,000 peso forced loan from merchants. He then chartered ten ships and embarked 1,000 infantry. Throwing aside all caution and legal restraint, he sailed north—without regard to either the whereabouts of the Spanish navy or the constitutional statute that required him to obtain permission for the troops from the state of Vera Cruz to enter the state of Tamaulipas. Santa Anna had no way of knowing that the Spanish governor of Cuba had ordered the fleet to return immediately once the troops had landed or that General Barradas and Admiral Laborde argued incessantly. Santa Anna ordered 1,000 cavalrymen to ride north and join him south of Tampico.[2]

While Santa Anna was sailing north, Barradas moved 2,000 of his men north of Tampico seeking healthier ground. Santa Anna landed at Tuxpan ninety miles south of Tampico in early August, where he reunited with his cavalry. He sent his cavalry around Tamiahua Lagoon and used small craft to cross his infantry and artillery. The force again reunited below Tampico on 16 August. On the 21st Santa Anna attacked the 600 Spaniards south of the port. At two o'clock in the afternoon, the Spaniards asked for a truce. While these talks were going on, General Barradas returned with 2,000 Spanish soldiers. Although Santa Anna and his staff were in an awkward position, Barradas honored the truce and permitted them to withdraw.[3]

While these events were transpiring, Mexican General Manuel Mier y Terán blocked Barradas's route inland and assembled other Mexican troops at Altamira, some twenty miles north of Tampico. On 7 September, this force of 1,000 regulars, 1,000 militia, and 3 cannon joined Santa Anna's force. As the Mexicans grew stronger, the Spaniards grew weaker from the effects of yellow fever. Mier advised Santa Anna to order a bombardment. Even though time was on his side, Santa Anna sensed victory and craved acclamation. He attacked in the late afternoon of 10 September, and the fighting continued well into the night. By the close of the day, the Spanish force had been reduced by 908 men, mostly by disease, and the Mexicans had lost 135 dead and 151 wounded. Santa Anna accepted the Spanish surrender the next day. The surviving 1,792 Spaniards were permitted to sail for Cuba after surrendering their weapons and supplies. Santa Anna was acclaimed a national hero. Mexican General Mier proclaimed Santa Anna's actions "a master stroke of boldness."[4] Others presented him with a jeweled sword. His homecoming to Vera Cruz was celebrated by banquets, balls, and Te Deums (church services of praise). Congress bestowed on him the title "Benefactor of the Nation" and he was almost beatified. Santa Anna once again returned to his estate.[5]

An event now transpired which demonstrated that Santa Anna was not yet the master of Mexico. In late 1829 Conservative Vice President Bustamante rebelled against Liberal President Guerrero. Santa Anna declared his support for Guerrero, gathered a following, and marched toward Mexico City. Once again, he declared that he would fight to the death. But Bustamante had outbribed Santa Anna's troops, and Santa Anna had gone only as far as Fortress Perote when his men deserted him. Then he received the news that Guerrero had fled the capital. Embarrassed by having backed the losing side, Santa Anna returned to his estate and gave up his political and military positions.[6] He spent two quiet years at *Manga de Clavo*.

Having been declared president by Congress, Bustamante proved to be an unpopular "chief executive." Executing Guerrero, the old revolutionary hero, had tainted his legitimacy. Then an opportunity for Santa Anna to return to center stage presented itself. Colonel Pedro Telmo de Landero, who probably had been given command of the port of Vera Cruz because of his dislike for Santa Anna, gambled away 18,000 pesos of the government's money. Fearing discovery, he turned to the one individual rich enough to advance the money, Antonio López de Santa Anna. In exchange for the loan, Santa Anna required that Telmo begin a rebellion against Bustamante.

Telmo rebelled on 2 January 1832, and two days later Santa

Anna wrote to Bustamante offering to mediate on his behalf. Not taking any chances, Santa Anna seized 279,000 pesos belonging to the government and began raising an army without even waiting for Bustamante's reply. The government sent General José Calderón from Mexico City to deal with Santa Anna.

Santa Anna's army did not impress one English traveler:

> As the general's men had fought and conquered, they had a right to be called soldiers; but certainly heroes exhibiting so unmilitary and extraordinary an appearance, I have never witnessed before. They were attired in shreds and patches formed of every color in the rainbow. Some had no uniforms at all. . . . The cavalry, so to call them, were a complete mob of half-starved peasantry. . . . Their accoutrements corresponded in fanciful variety with the rest of the motley attire; and rusty swords, broken pikes, and worn-out firelocks, apparently kept for show rather than use, constituted the mortal weapons of this ragged cavalcade.[7]

Appearances can be deceiving. These soldiers were the *jarachos* —the guerrillas of the coastal lowlands. They were immune to the bite of the disease-carrying mosquito and accustomed to the climate. They could live off what they plucked from the trees and bushes. Santa Anna was used to commanding such a ragtag army. On 25 February at the head of 300 horsemen, he captured a government convoy about fifteen miles from Vera Cruz. His prize was some 30,000 pesos. On 3 March, the two armies fought at Tolumé near Vera Cruz. Outnumbered two to one, Santa Anna was defeated, losing 450 men killed and wounded, including 32 officers. Among the dead was Colonel Pedro Landero.[8]

Santa Anna raced back to Vera Cruz and exhibited that boundless energy for which he became famous. When the cautious Calderón appeared before Vera Cruz, he found no fewer than 112 cannons and 2,500 men defending the walls. In spite of the fact that yellow fever season had begun, he lay siege to Vera Cruz. After losing 1,000 men to the dreaded disease, Calderón retired to the highlands on 15 May. Santa Anna had held out long enough so that the rebellion had begun to spread throughout the rest of Mexico. In additional, during the time Santa Anna had held Vera

Cruz, the port's customs house had collected 400,000 pesos in import duties; Santa Anna used these funds to finance the revolution.[9]

Now Santa Anna began an unrelenting march toward Mexico City, fighting skirmishes along the way. The closer he got to Mexico City, the more the other *caudillos* came over to his side. On 21 December, just outside Mexico City, Santa Anna demanded that Gómez Pedraza serve out the remaining three months of Mexico's second presidential term. Why Gómez Pedraza, whom Santa Anna had deposed in 1829? The answer is that his selection, at least in Santa Anna's mind, restored legitimacy to the government. It was Gómez Pedraza who in 1829 had been chosen by the state legislatures as required by the constitution, whereas Vicente Guerrero, who was now dead, had been the choice of the people as determined by Santa Anna.[10]

Antonio López de Santa Anna triumphantly entered Mexico City on 3 January 1833; Gómez Pedraza called him the "illustrious military genius of the people."[11]

Chapter 4

The Road to the Alamo

Thanks to the audacity of Santa Anna, the Spanish menace had been defeated and the "legitimacy" of the second presidency had been restored. If the past were prologue, the Liberals and Conservatives would sink back into their blood feud. Those who dared to seize the presidency from either side ran the risk of the firing squad once they lost control, which invariably happened. Such had been the fates of Father Miguel Hidalgo, Father José María Morelos, Agustín de Iturbide, and Vicente Guerrero. In such turbulent times, there was one who could lift the nation above these endless political feuds—Antonio López de Santa Anna.[1]

Few army officers sympathized with the Liberal cause. The Liberals believed that many of the nation's woes could be traced to the special privileges given to the military and the Church. The one prominent military officer whom the Liberals thought they could trust was Santa Anna. After all, he had proclaimed the republic, had sparked the deposing of Conservative Gómez Pedraza, and had orchestrated the fall of the Conservative Bustamante.

In 1833 Liberal López de Santa Anna won the presidency by the largest majority in the brief history of the young republic. He gained the support of sixteen of the eighteen states — only Chihuahua and Guanajuato did not vote for him. Valentín Gómez Farías, the intellectual patriarch of the Liberals, was chosen vice president by eleven states, a majority. For the first time, both the president and the vice president professed to be of the same political party — Liberal. Having won the prize, Santa Anna chose not to immediately claim it; he did not even appear at his own inauguration, stating that he was in ill health. Being president required long hours of drudgeries and the ability to compromise; these talents were not in Santa Anna's repertoire of skills. So rather than face up to his responsibilities, Santa Anna retired to his estate, *Manga de Clavo,* in the state of Vera Cruz, and left the affairs of state to Gómez Farías. From time to time, Santa Anna would appear in Mexico City and briefly exercise presidential powers. But he would rather devote his energies to his new hobby, the collection of Napoleonana. Items related to the French emperor began to fill Santa Anna's estate.[2]

Archliberal Gómez Farías immediately set his sights on his political enemies: the military and the Church. He reduced the size of the army and abolished the military *fueros.* The first major blow against the Church was to secularize education. Next the tithe (a tax paid by every citizen to the Church and enforced by the government) was declared illegal — what a person gave to the Church would now be a matter of his conscience. Congress passed a law that permitted members of the Holy Orders to forswear their vows. Franciscan missions in California were secularized and their wealth confiscated by the government.[3]

On 1 June 1833, General Gabriel Durán rebelled against the Liberal government. General Mariano Arista, whom the government sent to crush the rebellion, joined the rebels. Durán and Arista proclaimed Antonio López de Santa Anna "supreme dictator" (ironically, Santa Anna was the president anytime he chose to go to Mexico City and exercise the power). Santa Anna marched out of Mexico City to put down the rebellion. His troops "took him prisoner" and proclaimed him dictator. In the meantime, Gómez Farías had raised 6,000 militiamen, the new tool of the Liberals, to defend the government. Reading the mood of the people, Santa Anna perceived this Conservative rebellion to be premature and chose not to support it. He "escaped" from his captors and returned to the capital. Without Santa Anna's endorsement, the Conservative rebellion collapsed.[4]

Potentially, the attacks by Gómez Farías on the military and Church were death blows aimed at the hearts of two conservative institutions, and both were prepared to fight. Who would champion their cause on the battlefield against the Liberals? The response had to be the one individual who knew when those in rebellion had the potential to win, Antonio López de Santa Anna. In a legalistic sense, Santa Anna now led a *coup* against his own government, from which he had chosen to absent himself. The Church declared:

> A thousand times blessed the man who with so skillful a hand has known to return to God His legitimate inheritance. . . . His name will be hailed by all generations; young and old, virgins and children will praise him because all of us, not only through the might of his sword, always victorious in battle, but because of his religious piety and his true Catholicism, have secured the peace and liberty of our Church.[5]

On 24 April 1834, Santa Anna exiled his vice president, Gómez Farías, who in fact had exercised the office of president for more days than had Santa Anna. Santa Anna immediately decreed that state militias should be reduced to one militiaman for every 500 inhabitants. This struck at the heart of the Liberal plan to counterbalance the regular army by creating a large militia.[6]

Liberals in the states of Coahuila (which at that time included Texas), Jalisco, Nuevo León, San Luís Potosí, and Zacatecas openly rebelled against Santa Anna. Except for Zacatecas, Santa Anna easily subdued these states. In Zacatecas, Governor Francisco García raised a 4,000-strong militia army, most of whom were untrained.

Worse yet for the Liberals, their military commander, a General Andrade, had secretly agreed to betray the militia. He bivouacked his troops at a defensive site and, during the night of 10 May 1835, dismissed the sentries. Early on 11 May, Santa Anna attacked with 3,500 men. The militia, led by a German soldier of fortune named Harcourdt, momentarily rallied, but soon they panicked. Furious at the unexpected resistence, Santa Anna ordered all foreigners among the militia executed. Having won the Battle of Zacatecas, Santa Anna seized all the arms and public money; he then permitted his troops to run wild—murdering, raping, and looting—in an attempt to intimidate Liberals elsewhere. He even carved a new state, Aguascalientes out of the boundaries of Zacatecas.[7]

On 31 May, Santa Anna dissolved the national congress, abolished the federal Constitution of 1824, and proclaimed himself dictator with an advisory council of Conservatives. On 31 August, he sent his brother-in-law, General Martín Perfecto de Cós, with 500 men to Texas. This was the last remaining Federalist stronghold in Mexico. Santa Anna ordered Cós to maintain order but not to antagonize the Texans. Once Santa Anna had gained control throughout old Mexico, he would march north and deal with the Liberal faction there.[8]

However, the Texans refused to remain passive. After a series of skirmishes, Cós announced that he intended to drive all American settlers, who had been there fewer than five years, out of Texas; he also dissolved the Legislature of Coahuila, to which Texas had been joined. Before long, the Texans drove Cós into an old mission on the outskirts of San Antonio, the Alamo, and began a siege. On 9 December 1835, Cós surrendered and agreed not to take up arms against the 1824 Constitution, which Santa Anna had aborted but to which the Texans professed to be loyal.[9]

In Mexico City, Santa Anna boasted to the French ambassador, "If the Americans do not behave themselves I will march across their country and plant the Mexican flag in Washington."[10] A major problem was how to pay for a military expedition against Texas since the treasury was empty. Congress authorized Santa Anna to negotiate a loan. He secured 400,000 pesos from the European firm of Esnaurrisar—at 48 percent interest per year. At the unexpected conclusion of the campaign at San Jacinto, some of these bonds would be found among Santa Anna's luggage, indicating that he was to share in the profits.[11]

While these events were transpiring, Santa Anna was assembling a 6,018-man army at San Luís Potosí, 616 miles south of San Antonio, Texas. Santa Anna's strategy was to force the Texans to fight in open areas where he could employ his superior numbers. He advised one of his subordinates:

> Should the enemy present himself to offer battle, you will first of all examine the position he has taken. If it proves so much to his advantage you will avoid attacking him. . . . If the enemy should present battle on open ground, you will waste no time in forming the lines so that his fire and maneuvers can always be anticipated by your own. Your well located artillery should deliver the first destructive blows. The cavalry in two columns will attract the enemy's attention to the flanks at the rear, taking advantage of any weakness or negligence to support the action; a sound maneuver when the enemy's cavalry is no match for ours.[12]

To help inspire his troops, Santa Anna created the "Legion of Honor" for those serving in the campaign. The soldiers and cavalrymen were authorized to wear silver crosses, the officers gold ones, and senior officers double colored bands over each shoulder.[13]

Santa Anna began his march north in December 1835. Ramón Martínez Caro, Santa Anna's personal secretary, later described the march:

> They set out on their long march over deserts, in the middle of winter, which is very severe in those regions, without sufficient clothes, particularly among the wretched recruits who in the main were conscripts and were practically naked; mysterious because in San Luís Potosí the Commissary General of the Army, Colonel Ricardo Dromundo, brother-in-law of His Excellency [Santa Anna] had been given the necessary funds for two months' provisions for 6,000 men.[14]

By the time the Mexican army reached Saltillo north of the desert, supplies were so scarce that rations had to be cut in half even though the army still had to march to San Antonio, 450 miles away. General Cós, leading a few hundred men, joined forces with Santa Anna at the Rio Grande, 150 miles south of San Antonio, in spite of the fact that Cós earlier had pledged not to fight the Texans. Santa Anna's army numbered about 6,000 men, having lost hundreds on the march north but having gained a like number from those with Cós and other reinforcements.[15]

The Texans were in a state of confusion. The commander of the Texan army, Sam Houston, was attempting to execute a strategic retreat to the east but few would follow his orders. As a consequence, some 183 men allowed themselves to be trapped at the Alamo.

Santa Anna planned to surprise the Texans with mounted troops, but the scheme misfired due to the failure of subordinates to properly execute the plan. His army began arriving at San Antonio on 23 February, a month earlier than the Texans had expected. Santa Anna immediately hoisted a scarlet flag from the belfry of San Antonio's church, indicating that he would give no quarter. The Mexican artillery began a bombardment on the 25th. Those in the mission returned fire, but a shortage of powder soon caused their cannons to fall silent.

At 1:00 A.M. on 6 March, Santa Anna moved his men into position. At 5:30 A.M. 1,400 troops attacked from all four sides. The defenders shot down the first wave, which was composed mostly of conscripts. The Mexicans attacking the east and west walls were pinched toward the south by the intensity of fire coming from the mission. After a short lull, Santa Anna sent in his reserves, and the attack was renewed from the north and south. By 6:30 A.M., the Mexicans had overwhelmed the mission and, true to his word, Santa Anna gave no quarter. Santa Anna lost 78 dead (which included 26 officers) and 251 wounded (including 18 officers). Many of the wounded died from lack of medical care; but Santa Anna did not concern himself with the well-being of his soldiers. The Texans lost about 182 men on 6 March. Six prisoners were executed the following day.[16]

Santa Anna's attack on the Alamo was brash. He had sensed a victory that could be gained immediately at the expense of his men's lives. Instead of waiting for the effects of his superior artillery against the old mission and its defenders, he had pressed forward. Santa Anna was pleased with this apparently decisive victory at the Alamo, and he was not alone in believing that the rebels had been crushed. In Mexico City, Lucas Alamán wrote, "Señor Santa Anna has so prevailed over the Anglo-American colonists who have rebelled in Texas that we may consider the matter over and done with."[17]

The Texan army was in flight and all that remained was capturing it. Moreover, the Texans had been easily trapped for no apparent military gain to themselves. This must have reinforced Santa Anna's opinion, formed twenty years earlier, that the Anglos might be good fighters but they did not make disciplined soldiers.

The march from old Mexico to San Antonio had been difficult, and a respite was needed. Santa Anna was "wed" in a bogus ceremony to a young woman from San Antonio. After "honeymooning" for a month, Santa Anna sent his new lady to Jalapa, where she took up residence as his mistress, and he began to chase the Texan army.[18]

Chapter 5

The Road to San Jacinto

Now that the Texans were militarily "defeated," it was necessary to intimidate those who would be permitted to remain in Texas after the rebellion had been crushed, as the Zacatecans had been humbled less than a year ago. Santa Anna therefore ordered: that all foreigners caught bearing arms be executed as pirates, that foreigners not bearing arms be moved away from the border with the United States and the Gulf of Mexico, that all Mexicans in rebellion be exiled, that all expenses for the campaign come from the confiscation of property, that all land sales to foreigners be declared void, that all blacks be freed, and that the best land be sold to Mexican soldiers at one dollar per acre.[1]

Santa Anna dispersed his army in order to root out the American settlers. General Antonio Gaona led 700 men northeast via Bastrop to Nacogdoches. General José Urrea marched southeast toward Brazoria. General Joaquín Ramírez Sesma went with 800 men to San Felipe de Austín, and Santa Anna took 750 men to pursue the fleeing Texas government. All would reunite near San Felipe de Austín.[2]

Additional victories followed that at the Alamo. On 2 March,

General Urrea ambushed 41 Texans at Los Cuantes de Agua Dulce; most of the Texans were killed and the Mexicans sustained no casualties. On 20 March, Urrea captured some 400 Texans near Goliad. In spite of an appeal for clemency from Urrea, Santa Anna ordered all these men executed. The executions took place on 27 March (Palm Sunday).[3]

Santa Anna chased the Texan army and government eastward. By April he tired of the chase and planned to return to Mexico by sea. He later observed, "Our military campaign was a military parade; but to remain in Texas, perhaps forever, what a misfortune!"[4] However, the senior officers of his army were not so confident that the Texans were defeated and persuaded Santa Anna to remain a while longer. So Santa Anna continued the chase. He arrived at Harrisburg, Texas, only hours after the Texan government had fled; Santa Anna burned the town on 16 April. He hurried on to New Washington on Galveston Bay, arriving the next day just in time to see the Texan president board a schooner and sail away. While in New Washington, a scout informed Santa Anna that Houston's army was approaching. Santa Anna panicked. He mounted his horse and rode through his troops shouting, "The enemy is upon us; the enemy is upon us!"[5] Regaining his composure, Santa Anna explained that he was testing the readiness of his troops. Santa Anna burned New Washington to the ground.[6]

During this chase, Santa Anna, commanding 1,100 men, had outdistanced his subordinate generals and their commands; he ordered them to join him immediately at Fort Bend. Unfortunately for Santa Anna, Sam Houston had intercepted dispatches between General Vicente Filisola and Santa Anna and was aware that Santa Anna's force was well in advance of the bulk of the Mexican army. Marching hard, Houston closed the sixty miles separating the two armies in two and one-half days. On 20 April, Houston positioned his 800 men in the woods by the San Jacinto River and awaited Santa Anna's 1,100-man force.

Santa Anna, believing that Houston's army was trapped between two swollen rivers, was content to await the arrival of his scattered army. On the morning of 21 April, General Cós, commanding 400 men, arrived after having marched all night. As the day wore on, Santa Anna became confident that the Texans would not start a battle so he decided to rest. At 4:30 P.M., Houston attacked, literally catching Santa Anna asleep. The poorly disciplined Texans soon changed from an advancing military formation to a vicious mob. Awakened, Santa Anna frantically tried to restore order among his troops. The battle lasted 18 minutes, but the killing went on much longer; the Mexicans were ready to quit, but the Texans would not. Six hundred and fifty Mexicans were killed and some 730 taken prisoner. Among the dead was General Manuel Fernández Castrillón, who was the "officer of the day" and responsible for camp security; among the few Mexicans unaccounted for was Santa Anna. Two Texans were killed (six died later) and twenty-three were wounded.[7]

Santa Anna was still at large, and the remaining Mexican army, although scattered throughout Texas, was more numerous than Houston's. However, the drama ended the day following the battle when one Joel W. Robison rode into camp with a distinguished-looking Mexican mounted behind him. Initially, this person claimed to be a common soldier but his diamond-studded, fine linen shirt betrayed the lie. When shouts of "El Presidente" rose from the captive Mexican soldiers, all doubt of the identity of Robison's captive was removed.[8]

Santa Anna was brought before Houston, who was lying on the ground, his right leg shattered above the ankle by a musket ball. For the average general whose army had been destroyed on the battlefield, all should have been lost. Not so for Antonio López de Santa Anna. A political escape might yet be crafted from this seemingly decisive military defeat.

Initially, Santa Anna was unnerved and asked for, and was given, some opium. Once composed, he flattered Houston with praise for having defeated someone as accomplished as himself. Santa Anna, undoubtedly aware that friction existed among the Texan leadership, immediately suggested that he and Houston negotiate a political settlement. Seeking a common bond, Santa

Anna said, "I dislike to have anything to do with civilians, and would much rather treat with the general of the army."[9] When Houston pressed Santa Anna concerning his role in the death of the defenders of the Alamo, Santa Anna replied that the defenders themselves chose to fight to the death, which bore some truth. Concerning the events surrounding the Goliad executions, Santa Anna stated that he was just carrying out orders from the national government. This, of course, was an outright lie.

Santa Anna and Houston then negotiated two treaties. The first, a public treaty, agreed to an end of the fighting and the withdrawal of the Mexican army from Texas. The second, a secret treaty, obligated Santa Anna to prepare the Mexican cabinet to receive a peace delegation from Texas so that its independence could be recognized. Later when defending himself in Mexico, Santa Anna accurately pointed out, "I offered nothing in the name of the nation."[10] General Filisola, who now commanded the Mexican army in Texas, did as Santa Anna instructed and withdrew the army—in spite of the fact that Santa Anna was under duress as a captive when he issued the order. In return for these treaties, Santa Anna was to be immediately transported to Vera Cruz.[11]

Just as Santa Anna was about to sail, a Texan mob prevented the ship from leaving. Houston was away in New Orleans for medical treatment, and the remaining Texan leadership was unwilling to go against public sentiment. Soon, Houston returned to Texas and became president; what to do with Santa Anna was a challenge. Santa Anna, perhaps at the suggestion of Houston, wrote to the president of the United States, Andrew Jackson, seeking his help. Jackson by then knew that the Mexican government had repudiated Santa Anna and that he had no military or political standing. Regardless, Jackson wrote to his good friend Houston:

> I have seen a report that Genl St. Anna was to be brought before a military court, to be tried and shot. Nothing *now* could tarnish the character of Texas more than such an act . . . his person is still of much consequence to you, he is the pride of the Mexican soldiers and the favorite of the Priesthood and whilst he is in your power the

priests will not furnish the supplies necessary for another campaign, nor will the regular soldiers voluntarily march when their reentering Texas may endanger or cost their favorite Genl his life. . . . Let not his blood be shed unless it becomes necessary by an imperative act of just retaliation for Mexican massacres hereafter.[12]

Santa Anna bombarded Houston with correspondence. On 24 October, he wrote that the longer he was in captivity, the less influence he would have upon his return to Mexico. On 5 November, he wrote Houston that since Texas would never be rejoined to Mexico, the most critical issue to settle was the boundary between the two nations; this could best be accomplished with the help of Andrew Jackson. In late November, Houston allowed Santa Anna, Colonel Juan Almonte (his interpreter), and three influential Texans to travel to Washington. Mostly over land, the trip was arduous in these cold months. The farther Santa Anna traveled, the more courteously he was received. By the time he reached Washington, the Mexican *chargé d'affaires* was among the few who did not welcome him.[13]

Jackson met with Santa Anna and the Texan delegation. Santa Anna was at his best. He reminded the U.S. president that the United States had once offered $13 million for Texas. Santa Anna readily acknowledged that circumstance had changed and that this was too much money to expect, but that $3.5 million was not an unreasonable amount to pay to put the legality of the matter to rest. Naturally, the Texan delegation was admittedly opposed to such a payment, arguing that Texas was already independent. The issue of payment for Texas never went beyond the dinner conversation.[14]

Jackson ordered a U.S. warship to carry Santa Anna to Vera Cruz where he arrived on 21 February 1837. Not even Santa Anna could predict the mood of the Mexican people when he landed. He was escorted ashore by U.S. Navy lieutenant Josiah Tattnall; the landing party was met with a silent crowd. As Santa Anna approached, a military band began playing, a unit of soldiers saluted, and the crowd began shouting *"Viva!"* Santa Anna had not lost his charm.[15]

Ironically, the independence of Texas had done more to discredit the Liberals than the Conservatives. True, Santa Anna had waged the war as a Conservative, but the Texans claimed to be Liberals loyal to the Constitution of 1824. They proved themselves to be traitors by declaring independence, thus discrediting the Liberal cause. In addition, the prominent Liberal (and Texas land speculator) Lorenzo de Zavala, from Yucatan, further damaged the reputation of the Liberals by joining the Texans in their bid for independence and accepting the Texan vice presidency.

How did López de Santa Anna see the disaster at San Jacinto? According to Santa Anna, it was clearly the fault of General Vicente Filisola, his second in command. Santa Anna wrote:

> At two o'clock of a hot afternoon, April 21, 1836, I lay sleeping in the shade of an oak tree [legend says he was entertaining a young *mulatto* named Emily Morgan]. . . . The filibusters [Texan soldiers] surprised my camp with admirable skill, and I opened my eyes to find myself surrounded. . . . The responsibility for my capture rested solely with Filisola. He and he alone, had caused the catastrophe by his criminal disobedience.[16]

And in Santa Anna's view, Filisola's "criminal disobedience" was as follows: "First, he was not to send me any written communications which might be intercepted by the enemy [he did and it was]. Second, after joining with [General José] Urrea, he was to hurry his army to over take me [and Santa Anna claimed he had not]."[17]

The collapse of the Mexican war effort caused by Santa Anna's capture proved that he had become the *caudillo máximo* of Mexico.

Chapter 6

The Road to Vera Cruz

FOLLOWING HIS RETURN from Washington, Santa Anna lived quietly at *Manga de Clavo* for eighteen months; managing a country estate had to be a boring life for someone like Santa Anna. While he and the other generals of the Texas campaign wrote recriminating letters about each other, in the capital, the Liberals and Conservatives renewed their feuding.

About five years earlier, some feisty Mexican soldiers had destroyed a French-owned bakery at Tacubaya just outside Mexico City, causing about 800 pesos' worth of damage. As time passed, the French rolled together a number of debts and tacked on interest charges, finally declaring the total an astonishing 60,000 pesos. Such were the financial methods employed by powerful maritime nations against young, immature Latin American republics during the nineteenth century.[1]

In order to pressure the Mexicans into paying, France sent a naval squadron to the Gulf of Mexico. On 21 March 1838, two 60-gun frigates and four bricks (small sailing craft) under Captain François Bazoche arrived at Isla Sacrificios, a few miles south of Vera Cruz; however they failed to intimidate the Mexicans.

The ships were poorly supplied and the crews contracted yellow fever *(vómito)*. On 16 April, Bazoche declared Mexico's ports in a state of quarantine. Subsequently, Bazoche died from yellow fever and was replaced by the energetic, one-armed Rear Admiral Charles Baudin, who possessed instructions to use force if necessary. His squadron of four frigates, two corvettes, eight bricks, two *bombardes* (small sailing craft armed with siege mortars), and two steamers reached Isla Sacrificios on 26 October 1838. Baudin delivered an ultimatum to the Mexican government on 17 November; it increased by 200,000 pesos the indemnity demanded to include the cost of his naval expedition. Baudin demanded trade concessions as well. On the 27th, the Mexicans rejected the proposal; Baudin then informed the Governor of Vera Cruz, General Manuel Rincón, that hostilities would begin.[2]

In the afternoon of the 27th, three frigates bombarded Fortress San Juan de Ulúa from a location where only 19 of the 193 Mexican cannons could be brought to bear. The French bombardment started at 2:35 P.M.; as there was almost no wind blowing, the siege was at first hampered by the thick smoke from the Mexican gunfire. After 5 P.M., the Mexican guns fell silent, and the French guns continued to fire for four more hours.

To a large degree, the old Mexican fortress fell victim to a new weapon, the exploding shell. Although exploding shells had existed for quite some time, their fuses had been notoriously unreliable until the 1830s. The French exploding shells tore holes in the soft, poorly maintained coral walls of the fortress and sent debris flying in all directions as deadly shrapnel. Several Mexican guns were knocked off their carriages and two powder magazines exploded. The Mexican gunpowder was of such poor quality that the shot it propelled did little damage to the French warships. Thus it was a fight between modern French ordnance and an antiquated colonial fortification — the outcome was preordained.

When news of the attack had first reached Santa Anna at his nearby estate, he had rushed to Vera Cruz, arriving at 8 P.M. After he conferred with the fortress commander, General Antonio Gaona, and that of the town of Vera Cruz, General Rincón, they agreed that the fortress had to surrender and that the port should be declared "neutral" in order to save lives and destruction. Late in the evening of 27 November 1838, Generals Gaona and Rincón capitulated.[3] The French losses were four killed and twenty-nine wounded, while the Mexicans sustained more than 200 casualties.

Word of the attack reached Mexico City on 30 November, and the president, Carlos Bustamante, was furious. He declared war on France, ordered all French citizens expelled from Mexico within two weeks, recalled the commanders of the fortress and port to Mexico City, and placed Santa Anna in command of Mexican forces in the vicinity of Vera Cruz.

Santa Anna, who had returned to his estate perhaps not believing that Bustamante's reaction would be so extreme, once again rushed to Vera Cruz. He sent his aide, Manuel María Giménez, ahead with orders to close the gates of the port and let no one in or out. In the meantime, a party of Frenchmen, which included François Ferdinand d'Orléans, the Prince de Joinville, had come ashore under the armistice. The prince had returned to the fleet prior to Giménez's arrival and the execution of Santa Anna's order. However, a number of French officers were trapped ashore. As a consequence, Admiral Baudin maneuvered the warship *Créole* close to the city's walls and demanded their release. Santa Anna, appreciating the fact that he had nothing with which to bargain, freed the Frenchmen.[4]

Santa Anna was in a most difficult position. He was forced to notify the French admiral that the Mexican government had disapproved the neutrality of Vera Cruz and had even declared war on France. Playing for time, Santa Anna argued that neither side should commit additional hostile acts. At 2 P.M. on 4 December, Santa Anna held a war council with the ranking Mexican officers in the port. Although the other officers concluded that the port could not be defended, Santa Anna overruled them and ordered the defenses strengthened.[5]

In the meantime, General Arista and his staff arrived at Vera Cruz. He was being followed by 1,000 men from the "Army of the North," but they would not arrive until the next day. This was the first time that Santa Anna and Arista had met face to face since 1833, when Arista had rebelled to make Santa Anna dictator and Santa Anna had exiled him. Arista's mistake in 1833 was that he had been premature. They talked until three o'clock in the morning; Santa Anna convinced Arista to spend the remainder of the night.[6]

At 5:30 A.M. on 5 December, Admiral Baudin landed several hundred French marines and gunners at three points along the waterfront. Their objective was to capture Santa Anna and Arista, thereby hoping to preempt a general engagement. A column led by Prince de Joinville just missed capturing Santa Anna, who ran past a French marine semidressed. But the French did capture Arista. The raiding party began to attack the Merced Barracks. Arriving on the scene, Admiral Baudin ordered his men to withdraw. In the meantime, Santa Anna found his uniform and a white charger. He rallied some troops outside the city and attacked the withdrawing French. The French had positioned a captured cannon in one of the streets to cover their retreat. As Santa Anna led a charge, the grapeshot-loaded cannon fired, hitting Santa Anna in the left leg and hand and killing his horse. This broke the Mexican attack and the French quietly withdrew.[7]

The leg wound proved serious but not so serious as to prevent Santa Anna from immediately writing to the minister of war describing his "glorious victory." Santa Anna's interpretation of the fight was soon printed on broadsides, plastered throughout the capital, and readily accepted as fact:

> We conquered, yes, we conquered: Mexican arms secured a glorious victory in the plaza; and the flag of Mexico remained triumphant: I was wounded in this last effort and probably this will be the last victory that I shall offer my native land. . . .
>
> May all Mexicans, forgetting my political mistakes, not deny me the only title which I wish to leave my children: that of a good Mexican.[8]

Three physicians agreed that Santa Anna's leg must be amputated below the knee. The operation was poorly performed and Santa Anna suffered much pain, which reoccurred throughout his life. He was taken to *Manga de Clavo* to convalesce. One more time, Santa Anna was *the* national hero as a consequence of what would become known as "the Pastry War."[9]

Before long, Santa Anna had himself carried on a litter to Mexico City. The Bustamante government was being threatened by economic chaos and an armed rebellion in Tampico. The slow pace of Santa Anna's journey allowed him to gauge public sentiment. He arrived in Mexico City on 17 February 1839. If the Bustamante government were to survive, the president needed to deal with two challenges, one military and the other political: the rebels in Tampico and Santa Anna in Mexico City. Bustamante chose to first confront the rebels. As stipulated by the constitution, he wanted to leave the president of the Council in charge of the government. But the Council president was ill, perhaps a "political" ailment. Instead, Congress chose Santa Anna as interim president.[10]

Lost in the excitement generated by Santa Anna's return to Mexico City was the financial settlement with France. On 9 March 1839, Mexico agreed to pay France and its nationals $600,000 and granted most-favored-nation status to France, which was reciprocated. In exchange, France restored Fortress San Juan de Ulúa to Mexican control.

As once before, Santa Anna professed to be too weak to appear in person to take the oath for interim president so an exception was made. Santa Anna did exercise the authority of the office, suppressing the press and removing political opponents from key positions.

While Bustamante was in San Luís Potosí building an army, rebellious General J. Antonio Mejía seized the initiative and marched from Tampico toward Puebla, which lay some eighty miles east of Mexico City. Should the rebels capture Puebla, they could cut the National Road between the capital and Vera Cruz. Santa Anna asked for and received permission from the Council to lead troops to Puebla. He did not bother to ask Congress (which in theory held the authority), and he ignored the Council when it revoked its approval.

Santa Anna left Mexico City on 30 April in his litter. He was carried up and over the mountains that ringed Mexico City, arriving in Puebla three hours before the city's garrison was to declare in favor of the rebellion. Santa Anna's sudden arrival caused the would-be rebels to change their minds. By 3 May, Santa Anna had pulled together a 1,600-man army which met Mejía's army at Acajete just outside Puebla. After a bloody fight, which left 600 Mexicans dead, the rebels fled. Mejía was captured and Santa Anna ordered him executed. When told that he would be shot in three hours by order of Santa Anna, Mejía replied, "If it were Santa Anna I held captive I would shoot him in three minutes."[11] Santa Anna triumphantly returned to the capital.[12]

Once again interim president, Santa Anna took full advantage of the position. He gave out 2,000 promotions, he placed his supporters in critical positions, he moved additional troops into the state of Vera Cruz, and he issued new uniforms to selected units. In addition, 100,000 pesos disappeared from the treasury.[13]

Soon, Santa Anna tired of the responsibilities of high political office and wrote to Bustamante that he must return to Mexico City because the strain of the office was too much for Santa Anna's fragile health. The slow, plodding Bustamante, who had seven years remaining on an eight-year term, now had to govern in the shadow of the dynamic national hero, Santa Anna. Santa Anna retired to his estate. Bustamante did his best to satisfy the ego of Santa Anna while keeping him away from the capital. On 29 October 1840, the president awarded Santa Anna yet another medal, this one for his "victory" over the Spaniards eighteen years after the end of the War for Independence.[14]

The political pot boiled over one more time. On 8 August 1841, General Mariano Paredes, military commander of Jalisco, mutinied against the government of President Bustamante and proclaimed his "Plan of Political Regeneration." This was one Conservative rebelling against another. The movement spread rapidly. General Gabriel Valencia, commanding Mexico City's garrison, supported the rebels, as did regional *caudillos*, one by one. Finally, Santa Anna seized the fortress at Perote but professed loyalty to the government. On 9 September, Santa Anna proclaimed himself the mediator between the combatants and marched on Mexico City. Santa Anna met with Generals Paredes and Valencia and together they agreed that Bustamante had to step down as president. The three generals then competed for power, but Paredes and Valencia proved to be amateurs at this political game. Santa Anna entered Mexico City in a carriage drawn by four white horses and became president on 10 October.[15]

The vulnerability of Mexico's northern frontier was never far from Santa Anna's mind. He decided to reinvigorate the war against Texas, in part to justify a large army and to divert attention from internal problems. On 9 December, he ordered General Arista, commanding the "Army of the North Corps," to dispatch as soon as possible a raiding expedition of 500 well-mounted and -equipped troops against San Antonio. The departure of the expedition was delayed until 23 February 1842. Finally, 391 soldiers, commanded by Brevet General Rafael Vázquez, trekked across 188 miles during ten days of uninterrupted marching from San Fernando de Rosas to San Antonio. There, the invaders were met by 260 Texans, who, after negotiations, chose to surrender the city. On 5 March 1842, Vázquez took possession of the town, symbolically appointed an *alcalde* (mayor), proclaimed Mexican law to be in effect, and withdrew across the Rio Grande.[16]

Santa Anna was highly dissatisfied with Mexico's attack on San Antonio, stating that General Vázquez failed in his primary task "to take by surprise and capture or put the knife to the garrison of adventurers then occupying Béjar [San Antonio] as well as Goliad and Cópano, a blow that would have brought great honor to the Army."[17]

In order to counteract possible rumors that General Vázquez had retreated out of fear of the Texans, Santa Anna ordered General Arista to dispatch a force of some 800 men under the command of General Adrian Woll; to "raid on Béjar, Cópano, and Goliad, remaining for a few days in the first one of these places."[18]

Carrying out Santa Anna's orders, General Adrian Woll led 1,082 hand-picked troops, two artillery pieces, 12 carts loaded with corn for fodder, 50 young bulls for fresh meat, 213 mules loaded with 30,000 rations of flour and dry meat—enough for 46 days—out of Nogal on 31 August 1842. This undoubtedly was the best-provisioned Mexican expedition during the long struggle over Texas.

General Woll avoided the well-traveled roads and cut across the desert in order to avoid detection. He forded the Nueces River on 4 September, and on the 10th he camped some seven miles from San Antonio. Woll ordered the roads leading from the town cut. That evening a delegation from San Antonio approached the Mexican camp to negotiate; it was then the general learned that surprise had been lost. Woll immediately advanced closer to the town. At daybreak, he led the troops into San Antonio. Once the force had penetrated the center, it was fired upon. About 150 Texans had hastily constructed a redoubt in front of a house they chose to defend. After a thirty-minute fusillade, fifty-two Texans unconditionally surrendered. The remainder escaped through the back door and into the woods. The Texans lost twelve dead and three wounded; the Mexicans, one dead and eighteen wounded. The Mexicans gathered up 75 rifles, 22 muskets, and 72 horses and mules plus munitions. After some minor clashes with the Texans, Woll withdrew back into Mexico.[19]

In late 1842, an event occurred that underscored the complexity of Santa Anna's personality. Earlier, a small band of Texans had invaded Mexico as a reprisal for Woll's raid. They were defeated, and the survivors imprisoned in Fortress Perote. Santa Anna discovered among them the son of a Dr. Phelps in whose house Santa Anna had been confined while a prisoner in Texas. Santa Anna freed the boy and paid his expenses back to Texas. Also, Santa Anna learned of the bravery of a young lad named John Hill, who had killed several Mexicans in battle. Santa Anna adopted him and paid for his education. He also freed the boy's father and brother. Finally on 13 June 1842, Santa Anna's saint day, Santa Anna ordered the remaining prisoners freed. These acts of compassion were in sharp contrast with the cruelty he exhibited at the Alamo and Goliad.[20]

Santa Anna's private life was also complex. He had married Doña Inés when she was fourteen years old. She died in 1844 at the age of thirty-three. They had at least four children and rumors abounded of a fifth child who was reported to be mentally impaired. Forty-one days after the death of Doña Inés, he married María Dolores Tosta, age fifteen. At the time Santa Anna was fifty years old. Officially still in mourning for his first wife, Santa Anna did not attend his wedding ceremony in Mexico City but used a proxy. Nonetheless, the rush into a second marriage hurt his popularity. Santa Anna had no children by this marriage, but did have at least five illegitimate children whom he openly acknowledged.[21]

Santa Anna became increasingly egocentric. He walked out on a report that the Bishop of Michoacan, the government's minister of ecclesiastical affairs, was giving. When the bishop asked a presidential aide when Santa Anna might return, the aide responded that Santa Anna had gone to visit *Cola de Plata* (Silver Tail). When the bishop asked who that might be, the reply was: "Ah your Grace, *Cola de Plata* is the favorite game-cock of His Excellency and he is personally attending to its wounds for it has just won an important fight this morning."[22] The bishop resigned as minister.

Santa Anna's extravagances reached new heights during this era. His amputated leg was dug up at *Mango de Clavo* and reinterred in Mexico City with much pomp and ceremony, including a eulogy on 26 September 1843. Of course, Santa Anna was the guest of honor. *El Gran Teatro de Santa Anna* was constructed in Mexico City (today *Bellas Artes* now stands on the site); his presences were more loudly applauded than the performances. Santa Anna's statue was erected with his arm pointing toward Texas, which he vowed to reconquer. Those who knew him well remarked that the statue was also pointing in the direction of the mint. Money needed to be found to pay for this adulation. Import duties were raised by 20 percent, thousands of military commissions were sold, and mining concessions were sold to foreigners.[23]

Throughout this sixth presidency of Santa Anna, General Mariano Paredes had been courting the Liberals, who were becoming increasingly opposed to Santa Anna. On 4 November 1844, General Paredes, commanding 2,000 men, rebelled against the government. Santa Anna, once again semiretired at his ranch while others ran his government, gathered 7,000 infantry, 1,500 cavalry, and 20 cannons. On the 22d, Santa Anna set out for Guadalajara, 424 miles north-northwest of Mexico City, to deal with Paredes; unknowingly, he left behind a very hostile Congress.

Culminating a long series of grievances, Congress argued that Santa Anna as president had violated the constitution by placing himself at the head of the army. On 2 December 1843, the Congress voted a protest of Santa Anna's dictatorial conduct. On the 5th the capital's garrison declared for the Congress. Interim President Valentín Canalizo (Santa Anna's proxy) ordered the army to suppress the mutiny but it refused. A mob then went on an anti–Santa Anna rampage — it tore down his statue, it ransacked the theater that bore his name, and it disinterred his leg and dragged it through the streets. The leg was rescued by the minister of war and reburied — its third interment. Congress named José Joaquin Herrera as the new executive.[24]

Santa Anna learned of the rebellion against his authority as he marched north. He diverted to Querétaro 167 miles north-northwest of Mexico City, where he seized the money in the mint and extracted a forced loan from whomever he could intimidate. Those opposed to Santa Anna rapidly assembled a 15,000-man army in the capital. Santa Anna found his position increasingly difficult. His army was beginning to shrink through desertions. In large measure, Santa Anna had fallen victim to the grossly inefficient army he had created. Between 1841 and 1844, he had sold some 12,000 commissions into the army.[25] Paredes's army now at Guadalajara had swollen to 4,000 men, and Herrera controlled the capital with 15,000 men commanded by Generals Bravo and Valencia. The anti–Santa Anna uprising spread to the east and south.

Believing Mexico City too strong to attack, Santa Anna marched against Puebla in order to secure a base of operations. The city would not peacefully welcome him, so on 2 January 1845, he attacked. Although Santa Anna carried some outposts, those in Puebla refused to surrender, anticipating help from Mexico City. Perhaps losing his nerve, Santa Anna permitted the reinforcements to enter Puebla unmolested. One last time, Santa Anna tried to cut a deal with his opponents. He would renounce the presidency and go into exile provided that he continued to receive his full salary and that his statues and portraits be returned to their places of prominence. His enemies refused.[26]

Santa Anna then attempted to flee. He disguised himself as a muleteer but was caught by some local Indians. Unfortunately, they were from a village that had frequently been exploited by the owner of the nearby great estate *Manga de Clavo.* The Indians decided to cook him (literally) before collecting the price on his head. A parish priest intervened and saved him from the pot. Finally, in June 1845, Santa Anna was permitted to go into exile "for life" and sailed for Venezuela.[27]

Typical of Santa Anna's arrivals on and departures from the political scene, he announced the event with great flare: "Mexicans! In my old age and mutilated, surrounded by a wife and innocent children, I am going into exile to seek a resting place among strangers. Mercifully forgive the mistakes I made unintentionally; and believe me, in God's name, that I have labored sincerely that you should be independent, free and happy."[28]

Chapter 7

The Road to Buena Vista

ANTONIO LÓPEZ DE SANTA ANNA never reached Venezuela. According to his autobiography, he was so graciously received by the Spanish Captain General of Cuba, Leopoldo O'Donell that Santa Anna decided to disembark in Havana. Cockfighting, a hobby now bordering on obsession, became the excuse for remaining. Obviously, he could more closely monitor and influence events in Mexico from nearby Cuba than he could from more distant Venezuela. While Santa Anna was secretly corresponding with various factions in Mexico, war erupted between Mexico and the United States. In the balance was a vast territory, the ownership of which would endow the winner with the potential to evolve into a great power.[1]

Inside Mexico, Liberals conspired against Conservatives and vice versa to determine who would govern the nation. Making matters worse, within each party were factions that destroyed any potential for party unity. While the Mexican Conservatives, who had seized power on 4 January 1846, were focused on resolving internal party differences and fighting the United States, the Liberals, led by Valentín Gómez Farías, plotted their overthrow. A significant problem for the Liberals was that few military men were members of their party, and they needed a prominent soldier to champion their cause. After the exiled Antonio López de Santa Anna promised that all he wanted was to return to Mexico as a soldier to fight his nation's enemy, the United States, and that he would not become involved in politics, the Liberals reluctantly turned to him. Liberal Manuel Gómez Cosío best sums up the logic of asking Santa Anna to return: "I detest no man more than I do pegleg Santa Anna, but in spite of that I would gladly throw myself in his arms if he wanted to come back and fight the dangerous faction [the Conservatives] that dominates us."[2]

At the same time, a plot to assassinate Santa Anna was uncovered in Cuba and a Spaniard arrested. Whether this was truly an assassination plan or whether Santa Anna had contrived the affair to win public sympathy in Mexico is unknown. Nevertheless, that was the effect that it did have in Mexico City.[3]

While these events were playing out in Mexico, Santa Anna was busy in Havana covering all eventualities. In February 1846, he had sent former Spanish Colonel Alejandro Atocha, who claimed to be a naturalized U.S. citizen and resident of New Orleans, to Washington. Atocha met with President James Polk and stated that should Santa Anna return to Mexico, he would be willing to set the boundary between Texas and Mexico at the Río Grande and to sell California north of San Francisco to the United States for thirty million dollars.[4]

Polk found this an interesting proposal and pursued talks with the exiled Santa Anna. Polk sent Commander Alexander Slidell Mackenzie of the U.S. Navy to Havana, ostensibly to report on possible privateering against the United States. On 6 and 7 July, Mackenzie met with Santa Anna. The former Mexican president stated that he hoped for peace and, should he return to power, would negotiate a settlement with the United States.

Next Santa Anna suggested how the United States might conduct its military operations. Santa Anna suggested that the United States should seize Saltillo, Tampico, and Vera Cruz. He pointed out that Vera Cruz could most easily be taken by landing south of the port and investing (surrounding) it. Santa Anna then professed to be a reformed Liberal who believed in the rights of the common man and free trade. This was precisely what Mackenzie wanted to hear. The military advice offered by Santa Anna revealed nothing that the United States did not already know, but it gave additional credibility to Santa Anna's claim that he wanted to solve the problem between Mexico and the United States. In the end, Santa Anna had promised nothing concrete, but he obtained assurances that he would be permitted to pass through the American blockade of the Mexican coast.[5]

While Santa Anna was secretly talking to the Americans, events moved rapidly in Mexico. The United States declared war against Mexico on 13 May 1846. The Liberals began their rebellion on 31 July 1846, and its success was assured on 4 August when General José Mariano Salas, the commander of the Mexico City garrison, joined them. Santa Anna sailed from Cuba on 8 August; passed through the American blockade on the 16th thanks to instructions from President Polk to the U.S. Navy, and entered Mexico City on 15 September.

A leading Liberal newspaper set the conditions of Santa Anna's return to favor:

"We will say to Santa Anna, if you recognize your errors, promote the welfare of the country, pursue a course entirely different from your former policy and prove by acts — not words — that your misdeeds were not crimes but errors, then Mexico will forget the past."[6]

Santa Anna immediately perceived that Mexico was in no mood to sell its northern lands, so he forsook his proposal to Polk and chose to champion the war effort against the United States. On 28 September, Santa Anna led the 2,500 regular troops remaining in Mexico City to San Luís Potosí some 327 miles north of the capital where 4,000 troops had already gathered. He arrived in that state capital on 8 October.[7]

While Santa Anna was marching to San Luís Potosí to build a new army, the Mexican army, which had been driven out of

Texas, was preparing to defend the most important city in northern old Mexico, Monterrey. Santa Anna urged General Pedro de Ampudia, who commanded the troops confronting Taylor in the north, to retreat southwest sixty miles to Saltillo and make his stand there. Ampudia chose instead to fight at Monterrey.[8]

After five days of hard fighting (19–24 September 1846), which brought both sides to near exhaustion, Ampudia offered an armistice to General Zachary Taylor, which he accepted. The entire Mexican force, taking their small arms, six cannon, and a limited amount of munitions, withdrew leaving the city to Taylor. Ampudia retreated south to San Luís Potosí across a 240-mile wide desert, arriving on 17 October.

Santa Anna was furious with these terms. He relieved the senior officers of their commands; however, in a few days he suspended the order, perhaps realizing that many of his most experienced officers had fought at Monterrey. Now, in order to take the offensive against Taylor, Santa Anna would have to recross this most inhospitable terrain before fighting.[9]

Both sides planned their next steps. President Polk was very angry with Taylor for agreeing to an armistice that included an eight-week suspension of fighting. Political pressure was building at home against Polk's desires to take much of Mexico's north; he needed immediate battlefield victories. Polk ordered Taylor to abrogate the armistice. Reluctantly, Polk chose an assault on Mexico City as the only sure way to force the Mexicans to cede their northern territories. This attack was to be commanded by General Winfield Scott, a brilliant, arrogant officer whom Polk loathed.[10]

On the other side, Santa Anna assembled his army and hoped for an opportunity to strike. In the meantime, he desperately needed money. When Santa Anna left Mexico City in September 1846, there was a pitiful 1,839 pesos in the national treasury. Congress appealed to the states but little money came in, as testified to by the 75 peso contribution from the state of Oaxaca. At San Luís Potosí, Santa Anna implored, appealed, extorted, threatened, and seized — talents he had honed during years of political maneuvering. He, of all Mexicans, was best suited to the task of forging an army from officers, some of whom were there for personal ambitions, and troops, many of whom were forced to "volunteer." He pledged his personal wealth and took that of those who would not, including the church. Many Mexican Federalists remembered well his rampages through their states in the name of conservatism a decade earlier and refused to send anything. Absent were troops from Durango and Zacatecas.[11]

Everything was in short supply, particularly winter clothing. There was not enough gunpowder to conduct target practice. As in the past, Santa Anna lived an extravagant lifestyle while his troops suffered. Also, he devoted too much of his time to political intrigue and too little to preparing himself and his troops for battle. Manuel Balbontín described Santa Anna's army:

> The troops were drilled with frequency. The infantry, by brigades, under the command of its respective generals; but they never saw a general drill, not even by division. The cavalry maneuvered only by regiments. The artillery were rarely accustomed to maneuver and never fired blanks. The general-in-chief never appeared in the camp of instruction, by luck, because he could not appreciate the respective quality of the corps which were under his command. . . .
>
> During the months of November and December, reinforcements arrived for the army. Also, the troops raised in the states of Guanajuato and Jalisco arrived. These troops were in general badly armed; there were corps in which were seen arms of all sizes, and a large part without bayonets, one noted many guns held together with leather straps or with cords instead of braces.[12]

Santa Anna did have a few favorites among the units in his army. They were well outfitted and well fed while most others suffered without the essentials. The Hussars Regiment (elite mounted troops) was at the top of the pecking order. Next came the first, third, and fourth light infantry and the eleventh line infantry regiments. At the other extreme, the auxiliaries from Guanajuato, León, Celaya, and Guadalajara were among the worst provided for. At first glance, favoring specific units might seem to be folly because it created jealousies. But a *caudillo* needed to ensure the personal loyalty of his followers. Since there was not enough to go around, this policy of favoring specific units at least guaranteed Santa Anna the dedication of his elite troops.[13]

Santa Anna's political intrigue bore a hollow victory while at San Luís Potosí. On 24 December 1846, he was elected interim president and Gómez Farías vice president by the Congress. But there was a proviso: he was to remain at the head of the army, which under Mexican law disqualified him from exercising the power of the supreme office. Therefore, Santa Anna was president in title only and Vice President Gómez Farías was the real executive power.[14]

Gómez Farías immediately confiscated Church property, ostensibly in order to raise five million pesos for the war effort. Gómez Farías seemed more interested in punishing the church than in outfitting Santa Anna's army. On 27 January 1847, Santa Anna would write to Gómez Farías: "The government has sent no aid to the patient troops. . . . I fail to understand how your conscience permits you to sleep, knowing that since you took charge of the government (a month ago) you have not sent a single peso."[15]

Santa Anna soon received a dispatch from his enemy, General Taylor, stating that hostilities would be renewed on 13 November 1846. Santa Anna ordered work rushed on the defenses of San Luís Potosí, had the water towers along the desert road from Saltillo to San Luís Potosí destroyed, and sent strong cavalry detachments to scout northward for the Americans.[16]

At this time Santa Anna chose to order the port of Tampico abandoned. (Santa Anna preferred to use the name given to the town following his victory over the Spaniards in 1829 — Santa Anna de Tamaulipas — but most others used the old name.) Tampico lay 240 miles north-northwest of Vera Cruz and 180 miles east of San Luís Potosí. On the one hand, it was too far from San Luís Potosí to be supported should it be attacked; therefore to defend it adequately, Santa Anna would need to split his army, something he did not want to do. On the other hand, it was clear

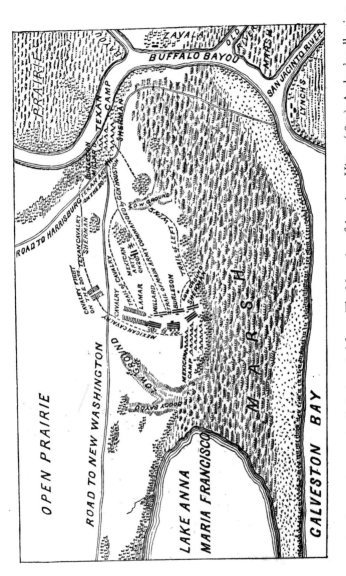

Battle of San Jacinto, 21 April 1836, copied from *The Magazine of American History* (1879). Author's collection.

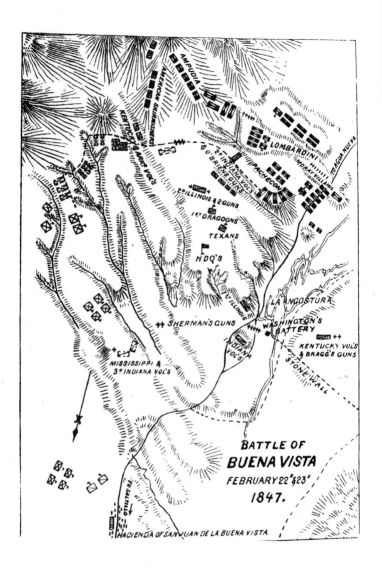

Battle of Buena Vista, copied from *The Magazine of American History* (1879). Atypical of most maps, north is at the bottom. Author's collection.

A young Antonio López de Santa Anna wears a style of tunic made popular during the Napoleonic wars. Note the hair combed forward in Napoleonic style. The Order of Guadalupe around his neck was awarded to him by Emperor Agustín de Iturbide in 1822. Copied from Nicolás León, *Compendio de la Historia General de México* (1902). Author's collection.

Agustín de Iturbide was the first emperor of Mexico. He created the Order of Guadalupe but had the gall to award Santa Anna only a second class medal. Santa Anna played a minor role in his ascendancy in 1822 and a more important one in his overthrow a year later. Early during the War for Independence, Santa Anna briefly had served under Iturbide. Copied from Manuel Rivera Cambas, *Los Gobernantes de México* (1873). Author's collection.

Vicente Guerrero, the second president of Mexico, in large measure owed his presidency to a rebellion initiated by Santa Anna in 1829. Following Guerrero's fall from power, Santa Anna protested Guerrero's execution as he had that of Iturbide following his fall. Copied from Manuel Rivera Cambas, *Los Gobernantes de México* (1873). Author's collection.

Martín Perfecto de Cós, Santa Anna's brother-in-law, to whom Santa Anna entrusted important commands in spite of Cos's limited abilities. Copied from John Frost, *Pictorial History of Mexico and the Mexican War* (1848). Courtesy of The UT Institute of Texan Cultures at San Antonio.

"The Surrender of Santa Anna" at San Jacinto, painted by William H. Huddle. Santa Anna is in the center of the painting, wearing the white pants. Sam Houston is lying on the ground as the result of a leg wound. The uniformed officer standing fourth from the left of the tree is probably Mexican Colonel Juan Almonte, who served as Santa Anna's translator during his captivity. Courtesy of The UT Institute of Texan Cultures at San Antonio.

American General Zachary Taylor neatly dressed in full uniform, not typical of his often casual and somewhat sloppy attire. Who was winning the Battle of Buena Vista between General Taylor and Santa Anna became moot when Santa Anna quit the battlefield on 23 February 1847. Copied from Cadmus M. Wilcox, *History of the Mexican War* (1892). Author's collection.

American General Winfield Scott was duped by Santa Anna out of $10,000 and perhaps much more. Scott paid the money to an agent of Santa Anna to bring about a negotiated settlement of the war with the United States. How much more, if any, Scott gave to the agent has never been discovered. The negotiated settlement never materialized. Copied from Winfield Scott, *Memoirs of Lieut.-General Scott, LL.D.* (1864) Author's collection.

General Nicolás Bravo had his share of difficulties with Antonio López de Santa Anna. Bravo was the commanding officer of Chapultepec Castle when attacked and captured by the Americans in September 1847. He accused Santa Anna, who was commanding the Mexican army, of failing to support him. Seven years later, General Bravo and his wife suddenly died after a visit by Santa Anna, who left an army surgeon with the couple to see to their health. Copied from Manuel Rivera Cambas, *Los Gobernantes de México* (1873). Author's collection.

General Gabriel Valencia was one of a number of senior Mexican officers with whom Santa Anna had very poor personal relations. Since many of these officers whom Santa Anna disliked were supported by constituencies that Santa Anna needed, Santa Anna could not simply dismiss them. During the defense of Mexico City in 1847 against the Americans, Valencia disobeyed Santa Anna's orders to pull back from an exposed position. Valencia's decision led to the disastrous defeat at Contreras. Copied from *Heriberto Frías, Episodios militares mexicanos* (1901), Author's collection.

General Pedro María Anaya hardly conveys the impression of a wily guerrilla fighter in this illustration. He refused to carry out Santa Anna's order to charge the Americans at the Battle of Molino del Rey on 8 September 1847. Anaya was the acclaimed leader of the revolution that overthrew Santa Anna's eleventh and last presidency. Copied from Manuel Rivera Cambas, *Los Gobernantes de México* (1873). Author's collection.

Valentín Gómez Farías, the patriarch of the Liberals, twice helped orchestrate Santa Anna's ascendency to the presidency, served as his vice president, and on both occasions, was ultimately arrested and exiled by Santa Anna. Copied from Manuel Rivera Cambas, *Los Gobernantes de México* (1873). Author's collection.

Lucas Alamán, the patriarch of the Conservatives, said of Santa Anna, "A combination of good and bad qualities; with very real natural ability but without either moral or intellectual training; a spirit with initiative; with both energy and a disposition to rule but handicapped by grave defects; skillful in making general plans for a revolution or campaign, but most unfortunate in directing a single battle. . . ." Alamán's untimely death on 1 June 1853 aided Santa Anna in his exploitation of the presidency for his personal aggrandizement. Copied from Manuel Rivera Cambas, *Los Gobernantes de México* (1873). Author's collection.

Mariano Arista wears the presidential sash in 1851. On occasion, he was struck by "political" lightning because he stood too close to Santa Anna. In 1833 Arista supported a rebellion that wanted to make Santa Anna dictator; however, Santa Anna, perceiving the movement to be premature, captured and exiled Arista. In 1838 Arista stayed the night in Santa Anna's quarters at Santa Anna's insistence. The following morning, French marines stormed the residence and missed capturing the fleet-footed Santa Anna but caught Arista. Copied from Manuel Rivera Cambas, *Los Gobernantes de México* (1873). Author's collection.

Santa Anna is honored by a *Te Deum* ("psalmlike hymn of praise and thanksgiving") officiated by the archbishop of Mexico in the national cathedral. Santa Anna is wearing the presidential sash and his artificial left leg is evident. Santa Anna alternated between being a Liberal and a Conservative to suit the mood of the nation. When a Conservative, he was generously financed by the church in order to protect its interests. Copied from Victoriano Salado Álvarez, *De Santa Anna a la reforma* (1902). Author's collection.

"Over his grand general of division uniform, Santa Anna was wearing his blue satin mantle lined with a violet taffeta bordered by gold-embroidered circles, laurels, and palm leaves. Big gold-threaded cords bordered by the same material tied the mantle.

At his neck he wore the necklace of the Order [of Guadalupe] consisting of eagle-shaped links alternating with laurels and palms, each one containing an 'I' and an 'S'— the initials of the founder [Iturbide] and restorer [Santa Anna] of the order. Hanging from the collar was a big golden cross with enameled arms in the colors of our flag, an ellipse at the center, and the Guadalupe image over a white background. An eagle was on the upper part of the cross. The lower part had a palm leaf, and an olive branch on the other side. Around the ellipse, the inscription: 'To heroic patriotism.'" Quoted and copied from Victoriano Salado Álvarez, *De Santa Anna a la reforma* (1902). Author's collection.

Santa Anna illustrated in his ultimate years of power during the 1850s.
The civilian dress contradicts the fact that in 1853 he anointed himself
with the title "His Most Serene Highness." Copied from Manuel
Rivera Cambas, *Los Gobernantes de México* (1873). Author's collection.

to Santa Anna that Scott was going to attempt to capture Vera Cruz. Should the United States take Tampico, it would gain a base close to Vera Cruz from which to carry out the assault. Yet Tampico in Mexican hands created other problems for the United States: it was very difficult to blockade because of shallows off the port. The Americans had already lost one warship there, the *Sommers,* in a storm. The choices were difficult, and Santa Anna made the most practical decision.[17]

Santa Anna's decision to abandon Tampico was criticized in Mexico City. He wrote to the vice president making it clear who was in charge of military matters: "I do not consider myself, nor should I be considered, by the gentlemen who compose the government of the country, as a mere General commanding a corps of the army, but as the *sole caudillo* of the nation to whom direction of its destinies has been entrusted."[18] Soon after Tampico was abandoned, the Americans occupied the port.

By December 1846, Santa Anna decided to strike northward against General Worth at Saltillo. Santa Anna had received intelligence that the Americans were planning an attack on Vera Cruz, and the American forces to his north under General Taylor were disbursing in an endeavor to gain political control over northern old Mexico. Santa Anna would march north with 9,000 infantry (his best), 4,000 cavalry, and 12 guns. However, when on Christmas eve Santa Anna received new intelligence that Taylor had reconcentrated his army, Santa Anna canceled the expedition.[19]

Luck now favored Santa Anna. On 6 January 1847, he was handed captured American dispatches, which revealed that all of Taylor's regulars, the best of his troops, had been sent to the coast to join Winfield Scott and the assault against Vera Cruz. Santa Anna chose a brash plan of action. He would strike at the weakened Taylor in the north. To assure that Taylor could not escape, Santa Anna ordered General Urrea, commanding 6,700 cavalry and irregulars, to capture the town of Victoria northeast of Taylor's location. This would cut American communications between Monterrey and Matamoros, the route over which Taylor's army was supplied.[20]

Santa Anna's marching orders made it clear that the army would sustain itself on the provisions captured from the Americans:

> Today you commence your march through a thinly settled country, without supplies and without provisions. Be assured that very quickly you will be in possession of those of your enemy, and of his riches; with them all your wants will be abundantly supplied. . . . The Commander-in-Chief commands, that the baggage shall not be carried with the army, nor shall the soldiers take their knapsacks; they shall carry nothing but their cooking utensils. All officers and other persons shall march in their places, and when bivouacking, shall keep at the head of their respective commands.[21]

On 27 January, the ill-equipped, inexperienced, 21,533-man Mexican army, dragging 21 assorted cannons, began trekking across the 240 miles of desert that separated it from Taylor's army. Santa Anna rode in a carriage drawn by eight mules. Immediately following was a train of pack mules, which, among other luxuries, carried some of his fighting cocks. To limit desertions, Santa Anna ordered that any man found half a league (1.5 miles) from camp be shot. Temperatures dropped below freezing and some 4,000 poorly clad men died or escaped during the march north.[22]

Taylor heard rumors of Santa Anna's march but did not believe them. He doubted that an army would cross the desert in winter, which is surprising since Santa Anna marched an army across the desert in the winter of 1836. Regardless, in part to help restore some discipline to his long-idle volunteers, he marched south to Agua Nueva. This pueblo lay seventeen miles from Saltillo, which placed Taylor about twenty-five miles north of the desert.[23]

By mid-February, mounted patrols from both sides clashed, but Taylor did not believe these events indicated that Santa Anna was on the march. The Mexican army, now numbering 14,480 men (which included 3,837 cavalrymen), marched out of the desert on 18 February. On the 20th, American scouts discovered the Mexican army and accurately estimated its size. Taylor ordered his army to pull back fourteen miles to the Angostura

Pass. Taylor left the Arkansas mounted men commanded by Colonel Archibald Yell behind to evacuate supplies and cover the army's withdrawal. At about midnight of the 20th, the Mexicans drove in Yell's pickets (advanced outposts). His men panicked, burnt the supplies, and fled. Santa Anna interpreted these actions as evidence that the entire American Army was in flight.

On 21 February 1847, Santa Anna ordered his exhausted army to draw three days' rations and to make a forced march across the thirty-five miles of wasteland that separated the Mexican army from the "fleeing" Americans:[24]

> The different corps shall today receive from the commissary three days' rations; and that they require the necessary meat this afternoon for the first meal tomorrow, which the troops are directed to eat one hour before taking up the line of march; and the second will be taken in their haversacks, to be eaten in the night wherever they may halt. There will be no fires permitted, neither will signal be made by any military instrument of music, the movement at early daybreak on the morning of the 22nd having to be made in the most profound silence. The troops will drink all the water they can before the marching, and will take with them all they can possibly carry; they will economize the water all they can, for we shall encamp without water, and shall not arrive at it until the following day. The chiefs of the corps will pay much, much, much attention to this last instruction.[25]

Santa Anna prohibited campfires that night, but it was so cold that many disobeyed. Regardless, few were able to sleep.[26]

At Angostura, Taylor ordered Wool to make the disposition of the American troops since Wool had had the opportunity to reconnoiter the ground and Taylor had not. Leaving Wool to await the Mexican army, Taylor led a few units five miles north back to Saltillo to help prepare the defenses against enemy cavalry that might circle the battlefield.[27]

Angostura Pass was an excellent, although not impregnable, defensive position. At that point, the Encantada Valley, which was some two miles wide, narrowed to a few hundred yards. The road leading northward through the valley paralleled the valley's western side, and a stream ran along its edge. General Wool blocked the road with two wagons filled with stones and placed five artillery pieces nearby. These were supported by troops on nearby high ground. On the American far left (the east side), the Kentuckian and Arkansan mounted troops filled the gap between the infantry and the mountains. On the right (the west side), a maze of *arroyos* (deep gullies) prevented the American flank from being turned. In fact, there was a route around the American right flank but apparently neither Santa Anna nor Taylor had discovered it.[28]

Santa Anna was continuing to rush after the "fleeing" Americans when suddenly, at 9 A.M., 22 February 1847, he came upon the American Army arrayed for battle. Santa Anna was in an awkward position. He was with the van of this army, which only included four light infantry battalions and 1,500 cavalry; his horsemen would have little use in the *arroyo-* scarred terrain. The remainder of his army was strung out behind him over many miles. In order to win desperately needed time, Santa Anna sent General Pedro Vanderlinden to demand Taylor's surrender, fully knowing what the answer would be. Taylor, who had rejoined his army, refused. This ploy won Santa Anna time to bring up his army; in reality, Taylor had no thoughts of abandoning his strong defensive position and attacking Santa Anna's strung-out army.[29]

Santa Anna deployed his forces as they arrived; the process took four hours. In the center he placed infantry commanded by Generals Manuel Lombardini and Francisco Pacheco; fourteen cannons supported these troops. On the Mexican left, which looked down the road blocked by the wagons, he placed three heavy 16 pounders and the elite Regiment of Engineers commanded by Colonel Santiago Blanco. Santa Anna himself chose the sites for these three heavy guns. On the right he placed his light infantry *(cuerpo ligero)* commanded by General Ampudia. Santa Anna, with his personal guard and the reserves, was in the center behind the infantry.[30]

Santa Anna launched his attack at 1 P.M. on 22 February. First, he feinted an attack against the American right. Next, he ordered General Ampudia, leading four battalions of light infantry, to attack the American left. The high ground on the left was held by a small number of Americans armed with rifles. These weapons possessed a much greater range (400 yards compared to 100 yards) than the Mexican muskets. The Mexicans pressed forward sustaining moderate casualties in a pouring rain. The Mexican infantry held the ground it won throughout the night without campfires or food.[31]

During the evening, Santa Anna reinforced Ampudia with 2,000 troops and moved five 8 pounders to high ground about 800 yards from the American position. He renewed the battle at 2 A.M. on 23 February by driving in the American pickets. Ampudia's troops renewed their attack on the American left, and the Americans gave ground. At 9 A.M. Santa Anna ordered General Ignacio Mora y Villamil, commanding the finest regiments in the army, to advance down the Saltillo-Monterrey road and capture Angostura Pass, which ran through the American right. This attack broke under the fire of the American artillery. At about the same time, Santa Anna ordered the divisions commanded by Generals Lombardini and Pacheco to attack Taylor's center. At this point, the Second Indiana Regiment, under heavy attack from Mora y Villamil, broke and ran. On the American side, General Wool reacted and immediately swung his artillery around to help plug the breach. In addition, the Mississippi Rifles, commanded by Colonel Jefferson Davis, arrived on the battlefield from Saltillo and immediately counterattacked the advancing Mexican troops.[32]

While the fighting continued in the center, the Mexican cavalry, some 3,000-strong led by General Anastasio Torrejón, turned the American left flank and rushed toward the American baggage train which was at the *hacienda Buena Vista.* Major William Bliss told Taylor that the battle was lost. Taylor replied, "I know it, but the volunteers don't know it. Let them alone, we'll see what they can do."[33]

Torrejón's cavalry change was met by onrushing Kentuckian and Arkansan mounted troops. The fighting immediately became hand to hand. Torrejón was seriously wounded, and the commander of the Arkansas troops, Colonel Yell, was killed in the opening minutes. This element of the Mexican cavalry was armed with *escopetas* (cut-down "Brown Bess" *musketoons*) and edged weapons, whereas many of the Americans possessed pistols in addition to their long arms. Grudgingly, the Mexicans gave way and retreated.[34]

While Torrejón's cavalry was fighting the Kentuckians and Arkansans, another Mexican cavalry unit, armed only with lances and sabers, prepared to charge the Mississippi Rifles. Before the Mexicans could effect a change, the Mississippians tore the Mexican cavalry to pieces with their long-range rifles. The cavalry retreated into a ravine where it appeared they would become target practice for the rifle-armed Americans. Seizing the moment, Lieutenant José María Montoya and three other officers galloped toward the Americans under a white flag. The lieutenant was escorted to Taylor, where, in the name of Santa Anna, the young officer demanded to know what Taylor wanted. Confused, Taylor dispatched Wool to confer with Santa Anna, but Wool was unable to approach since Mexican soldiers, ignorant of the ploy, continued shooting. While these events were transpiring, the trapped Mexican cavalry made its escape.[35]

Santa Anna collected men from various units that had been mauled, and under the cover of his artillery, which had moved forward, attacked the American left. The Illinois Regiment charged in an attempt to capture the Mexican cannon. The Mexicans, led by Santa Anna in person, overwhelmed the American regiment and drove them back with heavy casualties. Santa Anna had one horse shot from under him but mounted another.[36]

The reinvigorated Mexican infantry pressed forward. It captured the cannons commanded by Captain John P. J. O'Brien, who had chosen to make a stand rather than retreat in order to buy the American Army time. Next, the advancing Mexicans came upon Lieutenant Braxton Bragg's battery. Taylor ordered, "Maintain the position at all hazards!"[37] Other Americans soon joined Bragg's artillerymen. Finally, the Mexican attack broke.[38]

While the fighting raged, Santa Anna ordered General José

Miñón leading 1,200 cavalrymen to circle the battlefield and capture Saltillo in order to cut off the American line of retreat. The cavalrymen, armed only with lances and sabers, were no match for the American defenders. The battlefield was now drenched by an unseasonable downpour.[39]

By the end of the second day, 23 February, both sides were exhausted and they disengaged; they had each sustained heavy casualties. The Mexicans had lost 591 men (including 21 officers), 1,037 were wounded, and 1,854 missing. The Americans had lost 267 men (including 28 officers) and had 356 wounded and 23 missing; two guns and some flags were also gone.[40]

Unexpectedly, later on 23 February, Santa Anna ordered his army to fall back ten miles, abandoning hundreds of wounded to their fate. Santa Anna had inexplicably quit the fight. He ordered the campfires to be kept burning throughout the night and his exhausted army to march back across the desert. While this shattered army dragged itself back toward San Luís Potosí, Santa Anna went on ahead. A Mexican officer described the retreat:

> The food in the days before had been reduced to detestable and putrid meat, and the water which they drank was brackish. Those who had taken these unhealthy ailments were attacked with violent dysentery, which spread with a gloomy prevalence until very few were free from it. . . . The army seemed made up of dead men; the miserable condition to which the sick were reduced caused their skin to stick to their bones, and its shrinking exposed their teeth, giving to the countenance the expression of a forced laugh, which filled one with horror.[41]

The Mexican army staggered into San Luís Potosí on 12 March, ending a forty-day campaign during which they had received little rest. Santa Anna had lost 10,000 men to all causes.[42]

Santa Anna's decision to attack Taylor in the north rather than ignoring Taylor and awaiting Scott in the southeast was indeed reckless. Santa Anna knew from captured dispatches that Taylor would not take the offensive. Defeating Taylor would have given Santa Anna little strategic advantage; Santa Anna's army would have been in no condition to exploit a victory over Taylor for months to come. Rather, delaying Winfield Scott would have better served the Mexican cause. Should the war be prolonged, those opposed to Polk's expansionist desires might have gained political strength and possibly impacted on the outcome. Santa Anna preferred to recklessly gamble the most valuable asset that Mexico possessed, its army, at San Luís Potosí.

Why Santa Anna chose to end the Battle of Buena Vista (called Angostura by the Mexicans) following the second day of fighting will remain a mystery. Some suggest that he appreciated that his army was exhausted and could not continue the fight. But when had Santa Anna ever shown compassion for the well-being of his soldiers? Also, by quitting the fight, he had subjected his exhausted army to that horrific retreat across the desert, which would not have been immediately necessary if the Mexican army had continued the battle and had won.[43]

And how did Santa Anna describe the outcome? He wrote to Gómez Farías a few days after the battle, "Mr. Taylor remains in Angostura so frightened and destroyed that he cannot move in any direction."[44]

Chapter 8

The Road to Cerro Gordo

N o sooner had Santa Anna turned his back on Buena Vista and his hundreds of wounded who were littering the battlefield, than he learned of a Conservative revolt in the capital against his Liberal government. On 22 February 1847, when it had become increasingly obvious that the Americans would soon land in Vera Cruz, Vice President Gómez Frías had ordered five National Guard battalions, recruited from among the skilled and upper classes of Mexico City, to march within twenty-four hours to the defense of Vera Cruz. On 28 February, these battalions revolted by refusing to go and rampaging through the city. (They became known as *Polkos,* allegedly because they enjoyed dancing the polka.) The revolt against the Liberals was financed by the Church, an archenemy of Gómez Frías.[1]

Santa Anna rushed to Mexico City with the Hussar Regiment and restored order. But first he dispatched 4,000 infantry, two batteries of artillery, and a squadron of cavalry after four days' rest to block the road between the port of Vera Cruz and the capital. Santa Anna believed it critical to hold the American Army in the disease-infested lowlands. It was now late February, and hot weather was approaching; with it came the increased potential for yellow fever.[2]

Santa Anna's need for money was as great as his need for experienced soldiers. The Church offered him 2 million pesos if he repealed the anticlerical laws. For Santa Anna this meant that he had to sacrifice the Liberals in order to be able to continue the war, and he did just that. Once again he betrayed Gómez Frías; he even abolished the office of vice president.[3] Discipline was restored to the mutinous National Guard battalions.

In early April, Santa Anna joined the army at Jalapa, his birthplace, bringing with him 7,000 troops, mostly raw recruits. Many suffered from bronchial and intestinal ailments; most were infested with lice. Nevertheless, Santa Anna worked an organizational miracle creating yet another field army.[4]

Santa Anna chose to fight Winfield Scott at a narrow pass called Cerro Gordo, 4,680 feet above sea level, through which the National Road passed before reaching Jalapa. If Santa Anna could hold the pass, the Americans would be trapped in the unhealthy lowlands, which would become increasingly so as the disease-carrying mosquitos multiplied during the hot summer months.[5]

The narrow pass Santa Anna chose to defend was about one mile long and ran east to west. North of the road was the 500-foot-high El Telégrafo hill. Santa Anna placed four 4 pounders and 100 men atop the hill. At another hill to the northeast, La Atalaya, Santa Anna chose to place only a few men. South of the road was a hill that possessed three summits. Here he placed nineteen guns and 1,800 infantry. Across the mouth of the ravine just east of El Telégrafo hill, Santa Anna placed six cannon supported by 900 men. He held the 500-man elite Hussars in local reserve. The remainder of the Mexican army, including the cavalry, was retained in the main camp at the village of Cerro Gordo. Mexican engineers told Santa Anna of the possibility of a flank attack via a narrow path on his left (to the north), but he brushed aside their observation, stating that the use of the route was impossible.[6]

While preparing to meet the Americans, Santa Anna was

bombarded with reports of rebellion in Mexico City. On 7 April, Santa Anna responded, "Let the Government provide for the defense of the capital. I can attend only to this road."[7]

On 12 April 2, 600 American soldiers, commanded by General David Twiggs, arrived at Cerro Gordo. Twiggs, not appreciating the size of Santa Anna's army, ordered an advance. The Mexican gunners were overeager and revealed their strength in enough time for Twiggs to disengage. General Scott arrived on 14 April and ordered a reconnaissance. Captain Robert E. Lee and Lieutenant George Derby explored to the left and the right. Lee discovered the footpath that Santa Anna had chosen to ignore.[8]

The battle opened on the morning of 17 April. General Gideon Pillow attacked the Mexican right to hold the enemy's attention. Scott ordered the troops commanded by Generals Twiggs, James Shields, and William Worth to use the path to the left and get behind the Mexican position. They were to cut off the Mexican army's line of retreat. Twiggs left the path and turned into the Mexican position too early and attacked La Atalaya and El Telégrafo at noon. He captured La Atalaya, but the Mexicans held the heights of El Telégrafo. Santa Anna assumed the objective of the attack had been the hill and sent reinforcements. He did not suspect that the Americans were trying to circle behind him.[9]

The next morning, 18 April, Scott launched a general attack. Twiggs fought his way up El Telégrafo and turned the captured cannons on the fleeing Mexicans. Shields, using the path, successfully reached the National Road behind the Mexican position. Only Pillow poorly executed his assault against the Mexican troops defending the road, but this had no influence on the outcome of the battle. The Mexicans fled in disarray; however, Shields was too late to trap the entire Mexican army. Santa Anna barely escaped capture. By 10 A.M., the battle was over. The Mexicans lost some 3,000 men; another 3,000 were captured, including five generals. The Americans' casualties were 63 dead and 367 wounded. Among the trophies seized by the Americans was Santa Anna's wooden leg (he possessed spares). This was displayed for years in the Illinois state capitol.[10]

Santa Anna's strategy was a debacle. Foremost, he chose the worst possible site to fight. Given the geographical confines of the battlefield, Santa Anna could not employ his entire army. Thousands of men waited a few miles from the fighting in the main camp at the village of Cerro Gordo, which was the nearest site where sufficient water could be acquired. Also, because of the ruggedness of the terrain, Santa Anna could not use his cavalry nor could he rapidly redeploy his artillery. Second, the troops and artillery deployed were placed atop promontories where they could not support each other. This meant that the battle would evolve into fighting among smaller units acting under local command. The training of the American officer corps was far superior to that of the Mexicans, and such a fight gave the Americans a distinct advantage. Third, engaging the Americans before they escaped the fever-infested plains also subjected Santa Anna's troops, many of whom were from the highlands, to the same risks.[11]

Finally, it is unforgivable that Santa Anna was so brash as to dismiss the intelligence from his engineers that his position could be flanked. If any Mexican military officer should have known this terrain, it was Antonio López de Santa Anna. He was born near the site of the battle, he campaigned in this area throughout his career, and he may have even owned the land upon which the battle was fought.[12]

José Ramírez, a member of the Mexican legislature, wrote: "Everything is lost. Absolutely nothing was saved; not even hope. . . ."[13] Cerro Gordo may well have been the decisive battle of the war against the United States. Mexico lost the potential to exploit its most promising ally — the disease-carrying mosquitos of the lowlands.

Chapter 9

The Road to Mexico City

S ANTA ANNA RACED to Puebla to control the political damage caused by the defeat at Cerro Gordo and to create yet another field army. This city, eighty miles east of the capital, was the stronghold of the Conservatives to whom Santa Anna was now allied; however, they preferred that the stand against the invader be made elsewhere so that the city would not be damaged. On 20 April 1847, a suspicious Congress in Mexico City gave Santa Anna the administrative power to continue the war but prohibited him from negotiating a peace or ceding territory. On 19 May, Santa Anna finally returned to the capital.[1]

Santa Anna faced a daunting military challenge. As Representative Ramírez observed, "The army does not exist. What today bears that name is only a mass of men without training and without weapons."[2] Santa Anna now commanded only about 4,500 men. General Juan Alvarez was coming to his aid with 3,000 men, but these were irregular cavalry experienced only in guerrilla warfare.[3]

Politically, the lesser *caudillos* circled like jackals waiting to tear Santa Anna from the presidency. Valencia was in San Luís

Potosí with what remained of the "Army of the North." Bravo had "retired" but was nearby just in case the "people" might need him. Almonte was in jail, which was never known to be escape-proof. Only Ampudia and Arista had been knocked out of the contest by their earlier defeats. And the press wrote satire after satire:

> What a life of sacrifice is the General's; a sacrifice to take the power, to resign, to resume; ultimate sacrifice; ultimate final, ultimate more final; ultimate most final, ultimate the very finalist. . . . He is not alone in making sacrifices. For twenty-five years Mexicans have been sacrificing themselves, all of them in the hope that a certain person would do good to the country.[4]

How could Mexico City, inhabited by 200,000 citizens, be defended? The city lay in a 7,000-foot-high elliptical bowl (32 by 46 miles) on an old lakebed surrounded at a distance on all sides by mountains. Nearer the city were numerous shallow lakes, hills, lava fields, and marshes. Entrance into the city was gained over slightly raised causeways, and fortified customs houses (gar-itas) guarded their ingresses into the city. Santa Anna supple-mented these natural barriers with man-made fortifications. For whatever reason, he chose not to defend the narrow, winding road that passed over the mountains between Puebla and Mexico City.[5]

During this period, the Mexican Congress was in such a state of confusion that weeks passed without a quorum, making Santa Anna dictator by default. With tireless energy, he assembled and equipped a 25,000-man army. To obtain men, he emptied the prisons and impressed the artisans. But what an army—it was so ill prepared that it could not execute offensive maneuvers. Wisely, Santa Anna chose a defensive strategy whereby he would man the strongpoints with the inexperienced National Guard units and employ his regulars as a mobile reserve.[6]

Meanwhile, Scott had advanced from Cerro Gordo to Puebla. On 24 June, an English delegation had visited Scott's headquar-ters in Puebla for the second time. A Mr. Turnbull, a confidant of friends of Santa Anna, met with the American envoy, Nicholas P. Trist, who had been sent to negotiate a treaty ending the war. Mr. Turnbull said that Santa Anna was willing to secretly renew negotiations but that he needed to overcome the opposition in the Mexican Congress. Santa Anna also relayed that it was essential that the American Army advance no farther than Puebla and that money should be put at his disposal to allow him to buy the support of influential Mexicans. The British spokesman suggested that $10,000 in cash was needed immediately; that $1 million would be necessary at the signing of a treaty; and that the American Army should remain in Puebla.[7]

Bribing Santa Anna was outside Trist's authority and comfort level so he turned to Winfield Scott for advice and help. Scott agreed that the option should be explored and advanced Trist the $10,000 from the "military contingencies fund." By 17 July, secret negotiations with Santa Anna had matured to the point that Scott called many of his senior officers to a meeting and informed them of the events. He sought their advice on two questions: should he delay his advance to Mexico City until the arrival of reinforcements under General Franklin Pierce from Vera Cruz; and should he continue the secret negotiations with Santa Anna? All believed that they should wait for Pierce, but most were admittedly opposed to using bribery to advance the American cause. Scott thanked them for their frank opinions and adjourned the meeting without revealing what his actions might be.[8]

Within a few days of this meeting, Santa Anna's agents informed Scott that the Mexican Congress and many in the army still were opposed to a negotiated settlement. Santa Anna suggested that Scott advance on Mexico City in order to put pressure on those opposed to negotiations. Santa Anna was unwilling to take the lead in opening a public dialogue with the Americans; he feared the reaction of the Mexican people. Santa Anna and the Mexican Congress (which was ignorant of Santa Anna's secret talks) both declared that they would not initiate talks with the Americans. Neither was prepared to be held responsible for losing territory to the United States.[9]

Scott chose to advance toward Mexico City as soon as Pierce arrived; it is unknown if Santa Anna's advice influenced this decision. As the American Army was preparing to march, a third communiqué was received from Santa Anna. He now suggested that not only should the Americans advance, but also that they should attack the outer defenses of the city. Then the American Army should halt and await a Mexican peace delegation. General Gideon Pillow heard of this new proposal through Trist and sought out Scott. Pillow pointed out the dangers of agreeing to such a proposition. The following day Scott shared his reply to Santa Anna with Pillow. Pillow later wrote, "The note read something like this, that he [Scott] would not promise unconditionally to halt his army after he had carried the enemy's outworks. He might not be able to restrain the impetuosity of his troops. But if he could do so he might."[10]

On 7 August 1847, the American Army began its march from Puebla. Santa Anna chose to center his defenses on El Penón, a 450-foot-high fortified hill, seven miles to the east of the city. On 10 August, the Victoria, Hidalgo, and Independencia battalions, the flower of the city's youth, marched out of the capital for El Penón. Santa Anna deployed his forces as follows: he was at El Penón with about 7,000 infantry; Valencia was at Texcoco northeast of the capital with 5,000 infantry; Alvarez was behind the Americans with 3,000 irregular cavalry; and the Mexican reserves were in Mexico City. As the Americans advanced, General Gabriel Valencia marched to the southeast from Texcoco in an attempt to flank the Americans. In the continuing Liberal-Conservative struggle, the governor of the State of Mexico refused to allow the state's artillery and troops to be used by the central government, arguing that he needed them for the defense of the state.[11]

Scott neared the capital. On 15 August, he skirted El Penón by using a thirty-mile route through rough terrain discovered, once again, by his engineers, who included Captain Lee and Lieutenants Pierre G. T. Beauregard and George McClellan. On 17 August, the advanced guard under General Worth captured the village of San Augustín some eight miles south of Mexico City.

Scott had successfully flanked Santa Anna's exterior line of defense. Scott ordered Worth to advance north to San Antonio, which he found heavily defended. The American engineers reconnoitered to the west. They discovered that, with difficulty, it would be possible to cut a road through the rocky lava field called the Pedregal. Four miles in diameter, jagged red lava rocks sprouted out of the ground and little vegetation grew. Scott ordered Worth to make a show of force in front of San Antonio while the remainder of the army crossed the lava field to the west.[12]

Santa Anna hastily repositioned his forces and relocated his headquarters to the monastery at Churubusco. He intended to defend San Antonio and San Angel, which lay just south of Mexico City. He ordered General Valencia, commanding 5,000 men and twenty-three guns, to occupy the town of San Angel. On 18 August, in an act of insubordination, General Valencia moved forward to the isolated hill position at Contreras, ignoring the advice of his engineer. On 19 August, General Pillow's advancing division came upon Valencia's command and was driven back by the Mexican artillery. Valencia interpreted this as a prelude to a decisive victory. Santa Anna ordered Valencia to fall back. However, the overconfident subordinate ignored the order, and, amazingly, Santa Anna acquiesced. Valencia's insubordination had divided the command of the Mexican army.[13]

On the 19th of August, the American Army exploited a ravine that ran to the rear of Contreras. Scott ordered General Franklin Pierce to feint a frontal attack. On 20 August, the Mexican artillery opened a heavy fire in the direction of Pierce while American troops, which had traversed the ravine, attacked from the rear. The battle lasted seventeen minutes. The Mexicans sustained 700 casualties; 813 were made prisoners, including four generals, and twenty cannon were lost. Among these were the two 6 pounders lost by the Americans at the Battle of Buena Vista. The American losses were 60 dead and wounded. Santa Anna advanced with 7,000 men from Toro Hill but arrived only in time to meet the fleeing fugitives of the battle. Momentarily losing his equanimity as he was prone to do when under great stress, Santa Anna began striking at the fleeing troops with his riding crop.[14]

Regaining his composure, Santa Anna ordered all Mexican troops to concentrate along the inner defenses. In order to give them time to reposition, he ordered the fortified bridge across the Churubusco River, five miles south of Mexico City, to be held at all costs. The defense of the bridge fell to the 800-man "San Patricio" Battalion, commanded by General Francisco Pérez. This artillery battalion was largely composed of Irish-Catholic deserters from the American Army. They could expect no clemency if taken prisoner. The defense of the nearby Convent of San Mateo became the responsibility of the 1,400-man, poorly trained, and inadequately armed Independencia and Bravo National Guard battalions commanded by General Manuel Rincón. A large militia force under General Pedro María Anaya supported these Mexican soldiers occupying the fortified positions.[15]

On 20 August, the Americans attacked the bridge. Repeatedly, the San Patricio Battalion drove the Americans back. The fighting raged for three hours before some of the American troops were able to ford the river and outflank the convent, the defenders having exhausted the ammunition for their British-manufactured Baker flintlocks. Ironically, they did have ammunition for a larger caliber weapon, which would not fit into their guns. The bridge finally fell in vicious hand-to-hand fighting. General Anaya, dying from his wounds, surrendered to General Twiggs. Twiggs demanded the surrender of remaining ammunition. Anaya replied, "If there was [sic] ammunition, you would not be here, General."[16]

American dragoons (mounted infantry) pursued the fleeing Mexicans and attacked their flanks right up to the city's gates. Both sides sustained serious casualties. The Mexicans lost approximately 3,500 men, which included many of the remaining regular troops. Among the 1,259 Mexican prisoners were 85 men from the San Patricio Battalion. All were later hanged or branded. In addition, perhaps 3,000 men deserted the Mexican army. Since the beginning of the campaign for the Central Valley, Santa Anna had lost 4,200 men, either dead or wounded; 2,000 had been captured; and 3,000 were deserters. This left him with some 13,000 men. Scott had lost in combat 273 killed and 865 wounded, leaving him 7,359 men.[17]

The American Army was now but three miles from Mexico City and on the verge of victory. Santa Anna, commanding a badly shaken army, asked for and surprisingly received an armistice in order to conduct negotiations. General Pillow described the circumstance:

> The armistice was granted. Nothing was required as a guarantee, and after about twelve days of fruitless negotiations, during the greater part of which time the enemy was actively engaged by night and by day strengthening his fortifications and placing his heavy artillery in position, as well as collecting and organizing scattered forces, operations again resumed. . . . But the General-in-Chief [Scott] failed to avail himself of the fruits of this victory [battles to this point] which had cost us so much precious blood.[18]

During the armistice, Santa Anna called in outlying units and strengthened the fortified customs houses with earthworks. Scott reorganized his force. Both actions were contrary to the terms of the armistice.[19]

The negotiations led nowhere, so Scott terminated the truce on 6 September. Scott decided to attack via Molino del Rey and Chapultepec which lay just southwest of Mexico City. Santa Anna anticipated the attack would be against Niño Perdido and the Candelaria customs house, which were to the south of the city. Molino del Rey was a cluster of stone buildings that had been the principal cannon foundry for Mexico since colonial times. Scott had received erroneous information that cannon were still being forged. Chapultepec Castle had been built as a palace for the colonial viceroys and was being used as the Mexican military academy.[20]

At 5:45 in the morning of 8 September, Scott ordered the attack against Molino del Rey. After a brief cannonade, Worth led 500 hand-picked men against the position, which was stubbornly defended. The battle disintegrated into a contest between small infantry units where the Americans possessed superior leadership and training. Santa Anna ordered General Alvarez to charge the American flank with his light cavalry, but the general demurred, arguing that he lacked artillery support (true) and that his cavalry could not traverse a ravine that separated him from the enemy (not true).[21]

Aside from ordering Alvarez to charge, Santa Anna chose not to become closely involved in the defense of Molino del Rey. Apparently he believed the American attack was a feint and that the main effort would be against Candelaria, which was five miles to the east. As a result, many Mexican units stood around watching the fight and awaiting orders. The battle was costly to both sides, but the Americans achieved their objective. Santa Anna sustained 2,000 casualties plus 683 prisoners, and Scott's losses were 116 killed, 865 wounded, and 18 missing.[22]

Concerned over mounting casualties, Scott continued to advance from the southwest. Next he attacked Chapultepec. In fact, Chapultepec was not nearly as strong as one might conclude. It did sit upon a 200-foot crag; however, its walls were thin and by no means bomb-proof. This palace was defended by 832 men (mostly National Guard) and 43 cadets, some as young as thirteen years of age, serving seven cannon. The commander was seventy-one-year-old General Nicolás Bravo. To adequately defend the position would have required three times as many soldiers. Scott ordered Generals Quitman and Worth to attack the Belén and San Cosmé gates in the southwest. He sent Twigg to feint an attack against the San Antonio customs house to the south of the city. This last action reinforced Santa Anna's belief that the main attack would come from that quarter.[23]

Throughout the day of 12 September and into the next morning, the Americans bombarded Chapultepec with their heavy siege guns. At 8 in the morning on the 13th, General Pillow's division began the climb through a cypress grove to the base of the castle. It was temporarily halted by stiff opposition and only regained its momentum once reinforced. The American troops were delayed a second time by the lack of scaling ladders. At this point an American soldier discovered a canvas tube fuse, which led to land mines; this was cut before the Mexicans could light it.

After fierce hand-to-hand fighting, General Bravo attempted to surrender, but the cadets fought on. One cadet, Juan Escutia, reportedly wrapped himself in the academy's flag and leaped from the highest rampart rather than surrender. By midday Santa Anna finally realized that the assault on Chapultepec was Scott's main effort, but Santa Anna's forces were so scattered that he could not come to Bravo's aid. The United States lost 130 killed, 703 wounded; 29 were missing. Mexico sustained more than 1,800 casualties. These included six cadets killed, 3 wounded, and 37 captured. Bravo and Santa Anna began a heated and prolonged argument over who was responsible for the loss of Chapultepec.[24]

Scott immediately advanced on the city; Quitman's division was sent along the Belén causeway and Worth's over the San Cosmé causeway. Quitman ran headlong into the Morelia Battalion, which fought bravely until its ammunition was exhausted. Seventy-three-year-old General Andrés Terrés ordered his men to retreat to the Ciudadela (the city's arsenal). Santa Anna arrived with reinforcements too late to alter the outcome. Once again, he lost his composure, this time striking Terrés in the face while admonishing him.[25]

Scott had breached the inner defenses of the city, and the Mexican army was demoralized. Santa Anna, meeting with Generals José Alcorta, Lombardini, and Pérez, concluded that the city was lost. Santa Anna ordered the remaining 9,000-man army to evacuate Mexico City. He resigned as president but retained command of the army. Santa Anna was not ready to quit the fight, and no one else was prepared to take his place. He decided to attack the U.S. garrison at Puebla in order to cut the American supply line to Mexico City. His shattered army began to disintegrate as he marched from Mexico City to Puebla.[26]

The siege of Puebla began on 7 September by troops under General Joaquín Rea. Santa Anna arrived on the 22nd. He immediately tried to storm a defended convent with 500 men, but they were driven off. On 30 September, Santa Anna, leaving Rea and a small force to continue the siege, attempted to ambush an American relief column coming from Vera Cruz at Paso del Pintal. This also failed. Then on 7 October, the acting president ordered Santa Anna to relinquish his command of the army and to await a court martial which would evaluate his conduct. He retired to Tehuacán seventy-five miles southeast of Puebla. Santa Anna considered retiring southward toward Guatemala, but the Liberal governor of the state of Oaxaca, Benito Juárez, forbid Santa Anna to enter the state.[27]

The last insult to Santa Anna's pride came when 350 Texas Rangers attempted to capture him, seeking revenge for the Alamo. They reached Tehuacán on the morning of 23 January 1848, just two hours after Santa Anna had fled. Finally given a safe conduct pass by the Americans, Santa Anna chose to go into exile, this time to Jamaica.[28]

A disciplined Mexican army ceased to exist. The remnants of Santa Anna's army, some 3,000 men, were outside of Puebla. A similar number were on the outskirts of Mexico City, and no more than 1,000 men were en route to the capital from various parts of the republic.[29]

On 2 February 1848, Trist and Mexican representatives signed the Treaty of Guadalupe-Hidalgo ending the war. Mexico recognized the Río Grande as the international boundary between the two countries and ceded more than one third of its territory to the United States. As consolation, the United States paid Mexico $15 million and assumed the responsibilities for $3.5 million in claims by American citizens against the Mexican government.

Throughout the defense of Mexico City, Santa Anna had proven to be neither a gifted strategist nor tactician. However, his plans were sound and he deserves credit as the one man who was able to raise several field armies, find the money, the weapons, and at least some logistics to fight the invader.

Antonio López de Santa Anna was not entirely to blame for Mexico's catastrophe. In Mexico military success bred political ambition, which too frequently resulted in insubordination. The clearest example was the growing animosity between Santa Anna and Valencia. Valencia's actions at Contreras caused the collapse of the interior defenses of Mexico City. Obviously, Santa Anna viewed ambitious and talented subordinates as a threat. On the other hand, he had confidence in those who were loyal to him personally in spite of their lack of martial talents. His brother-in-law, Martín Perfecto de Cós, was an excellent example.[30]

According to Mexican Congressman Ramírez, Santa Anna perceived the inferiority of the Mexican officer corps. Ramírez wrote:

> I believe that poor General S.A. is suffering as much as I am today [3 April 1847], because, brushing aside all polite considerations, he said yesterday that in his profession all the generals, including himself, would hardly make good corporals. He said he wished most ardently that some of the Spanish officers among the Carlist immigrants [exiled Spanish officers living in Mexico] would apply to him; he would give them jobs.[31]

Santa Anna inherited other handicaps. The Mexican weapons were hopelessly inferior to those used by the Americans. The Mexican cannons were antiquated, the powder of poor quality, and the gunners inadequately trained. The most common Mexican muskets were second-hand European discards, which had seen their best years of service in some other army. Frequently, they were more lethal as clubs than as firearms. On the other hand, Santa Anna's misuse of public funds contributed to Mexico's inability to properly arm its soldiers.[32]

Santa Anna had counted on the more numerous Mexican cavalry giving him an advantage. But it was ineffective throughout the war. The cavalry's tactical experience was as an irregular guerrilla force; it could not be used to attack infantry and artillery deployed for battle because it was too lightly armed. General Alvarez's refusal to charge into the disciplined American infantry at Molino del Rey exemplified this. The Mexican cavalry's lightness, which was the source of its agility, prevented it from being used in direct combat against the American regulars.[33]

Mexico's internal struggle between Conservatives and Liberals significantly contributed to the nation's inability to defend its territory against the United States. Each accused the other of complicity with the enemy.

A question almost lost beneath the wreckage of Mexico's defeat is how much money Santa Anna and his fellow conspirators duped from Winfield Scott and Nicholas Trist. The answer is at least $10,000. The U.S. Army investigated the issue after the war, but both Scott and Trist refused to appear before the board of inquiry. Scott did submit a written account of his expenditures, but this was vague at best. Scott admitted to spending some $300,000 for intelligence from the "military contingencies fund." We will probably never know how much more than $10,000, if any, was paid to Santa Anna.[34]

One would think that the disastrous defeat of Mexico in the war with the United States would have forever extinguished the popularity of Antonio López de Santa Anna in Mexico. And yet, in the presidential election held on 30 May 1848 — only four months after the ending of the war — Santa Anna won three of the sixteen states that were eligible to vote. Santa Anna, in exile in Jamaica, was disqualified from participating by the Mexican Congress.[35]

Chapter 10

The Road to "Infamy"

By the 1850s, Mexico was in chaos. The United States had crushed it in a catastrophic war; it had to sacrifice one third of its national territory in order to get the invaders to leave. Many of the northern states were rebelling and talking of secession, and the Yucatán seceded for a second time since the founding of the nation. Banditry was common throughout the distressed nation, and French and American *filibusteros,* or "fili-busters" (soldiers of fortune seeking personal gain) invaded the north. These were soldiers of fortune seeking fame at Mexico's expense. Ignoring these ills, the Liberals and Conservatives con-tinued to fight for control of Mexico, which resulted in short-lived governments, a lack of central control, and civil disorder.[1]

While these events were transpiring in Mexico, Santa Anna chose to relocate from Jamaica to Nueva Granada (the future Colombia). There he bought a ranch near Turbaco, a small town fifteen miles from Cartegena. Simón Bolívar, the great liberator, had once occupied the house. Santa Anna loved to call attention to this fact and, in his mind, draw the "obvious" comparison between the liberators of northern South America and Mexico (himself). Santa Anna settled into administrating his estate, even building a tomb for his remains.[2]

Finally the Conservatives, who temporarily held power (for surely no one governed), called for the return of Santa Anna to Mexico in order to restore order. In spite of his well-known flaws, no one could deny Santa Anna's commanding presence and boundless organizational energies. Lucas Alamán, the patriarch of the Conservatives, sent the invitation,

> The first [of our principles] is to preserve the Catholic religion . . . it is necessary to sustain the cult with splendor. . . . We are opposed to the federal form of government; against the representative system through election. . . . We are convinced that nothing can be accomplished by a Congress and desire you to do it [govern] aided by councils few in number. . . .
>
> To achieve these purposes we can count on pubic opinion . . . which we direct through the principal newspapers of the capital and the states which are all ours.[3]

On 1 April 1853, Santa Anna returned from exile and became president for the eleventh time on 20 April. His cabinet included Liberals and Conservatives, which totally pleased no one; but for the most part, these were talented men. The most prominent was Lucas Alamán. Many looked to him to restrain Santa Anna from succumbing to the temptations of power. Providence dealt Mexico a cruel blow when, on 1 June, Alamán suddenly died only a few months into Santa Anna's presidency. All constraints on Santa Anna were removed, and on 16 December he was declared "Perpetual Dictator."[4]

Santa Anna rapidly returned to his old, corrupt practices. He repaid himself for the money he had loaned the nation during the campaign against Taylor in 1847. Santa Anna's lifestyle became increasingly opulent. On 12 November 1853, he reestablished the Order of Guadalupe; for enough money, anyone could be awarded the order. In order to guarantee his rule, Santa Anna increased the army to almost 100,000 men. He courted the Church, readmitting Jesuits into Mexico in 1853; they had been in exile since 1767. Santa Anna anointed himself "Most Serene

Highness," claiming, as usual, that others had suggested it. His excesses, already legendary, continued unabated.[5]

Santa Anna hunted down old enemies. He punished the Indians who had almost "cooked" him in 1844. He prosecuted those who had surrendered to the Americans in 1847. Santa Anna created a spy network to report on any disloyalty. He exiled any who spoke out against him. Those suffering this fate included such eminent Mexicans as future president Benito Juárez and scholars Mariano Riva Palacio, and Guillermo Prieto.[6]

The vulnerability of Mexico's northern border to incursions from filibusters continued to plague the nation. North Americans Joseph Morehead and the infamous William Walker had led forays into Mexico during 1851 and 1853. Santa Anna decided to invite itinerant foreigners (excluding North Americans), who were stranded in California, to Mexico. He hoped to create a barrier against North American incursions. Santa Anna gave permission for 3,000 foreigners to immediately land at Guaymas, Sonora. He planned to stifle any political initiative on their part by disbursing them in small bands among the coastal states. The Mexican consul in San Francisco asked the French consul, who in turn asked Count Gaston de Raousset, to recruit the men. The count had led an unsuccessful mining expedition into Mexico in 1852. Since he had been secretly conspiring with other French adventurers to return to Mexico and possibly declare Sonora independent, Raousset was delighted to participate. On 2 April 1854, he dispatched 350 men, mostly French, from San Francisco on board the British ship *Challenge;* the count remained behind. Raousset apparently had shared his scheme of conquest only with the other leaders of the expedition. The count slipped out of San Francisco on the pilot boat *Belle;* after thirty-five rough days at sea, he landed at Guaymas, Sonora, on 28 June.[7]

A cat-and-mouse game then ensued between Raousset, who was endeavoring to seize the port, and Mexican Colonel José María Yañez, who was trying to win time before reinforcements arrived from Santa Anna. Matters came to a head on 13 July when the Frenchmen attacked the Guaymas barracks. The Mexican troops held their ground for three hours while the Frenchmen, led by Raousset and low on ammunition, repeatedly charged their position. In the end, the Mexican victory was complete. Forty-six Frenchmen were killed and 60 wounded; 50 Mexicans died; 100 were wounded. At sunrise on 12 August, a firing squad executed the count in Guaymas's La Mole Square. Sixty of the Frenchmen were pardoned and permitted to sail to San Francisco. The remainder were marched under harsh conditions to the Perote fortress. With the intervention of the French government, Mexico released the survivors by the end of 1854.[8]

This victory catapulted Yañez to the status of national hero. Unfortunately, Mexico was apparently too small for two national heroes. Soon the colonel was accused of inefficiency and required to appear before a court martial where he was discredited.[9]

Santa Anna also proved to be jealous of dead heroes. On 10 February 1854, General José Joaquín Herrera died, and newspapers published complimentary obituaries. He had never been a friend of His Most Serene Highness, so Santa Anna sponsored articles attacking the accomplishments of the dead general.[10]

Regardless of the threats from the north, Santa Anna desperately needed money to guarantee the loyalty of his supporters both in and out of the army. Consequently, he sold the Mesilla Valley to the United States for $10 million — little did the United States know that Santa Anna would have settled for half as much. Known as the Gadsden Purchase (after James Gadsden, the U.S. minister to Mexico), the sudden wealth it brought, half of which he appropriated for himself, allowed Santa Anna to attack his opponents even more harshly. Another source of money in which Santa Anna shared was the sale of Yucatecan Indians to Cuban planters at 25 pesos a head. In July 1855, Santa Anna again approached Gadsden concerning the sale of more Mexican territory, but an uprising in southern Mexico overtook his efforts.[11]

Santa Anna had a typically unique interpretation of these events and the sale of Mexican territory:

With knife in hand, the Washington government was attempting to cut another piece from the body which she had just horribly mutilated. We were threatened with yet another invasion. Considering the deplorable condition of the country, I considered a complete break with the United States foolish. I decided to take the alternative which patriotism and prudence decreed—a peaceful settlement.[12]

On 1 March 1854, Liberals in the state of Guerrero proclaimed the "Plan of Ayutla" to overthrow the "Most Serene Highness." Among the prominent conspirators was General Juan Alvarez, who had failed to execute Santa Anna's order to charge the Americans at Molino del Rey. Nonetheless, Alvarez was an accomplished guerrilla fighter and not to be taken lightly. Santa Anna marched south from Mexico City with 5,000 men to put down the rebellion. He abandoned the old practice of traveling in advance of the army with a small escort and instead traveled in a comfortable carriage. At the end of March, Santa Anna stopped at Chilpancingo, 190 miles south of Mexico City, to pay a courtesy call on the old revolutionary hero Nicolás Bravo. Bravo still possessed a significant following; securing his endorsement, at the most, or preventing his supporting the rebels, at the least, had value. Seemingly, all was cordial, and Santa Anna left the sick old man in the care of an army surgeon. A few days later, Bravo and his wife died. Rumors spread rapidly that Santa Anna played a hand in their deaths.[13]

Rebel Ignacio Comonfort, who controlled Acapulco some 284 miles south of the capital, withstood an assault and, on 20 April, refused to surrender the port; this left Santa Anna without a supply base. Santa Anna burned some Indian villages, shot the few Liberals he caught, and, proclaiming the rebellion crushed, returned to Mexico City. His faithful followers built a triumphal arch topped by a statue of Santa Anna holding the Mexican flag to commemorate these "victories." Santa Anna, himself, was more realistic; he began stashing money abroad.[14]

Meanwhile, the Liberals slowly gained control, first over the south, then the west and north, and finally over the east. Santa

Anna twice marched out of Mexico City and twice precipitously returned. Desertions increased to alarming proportions. On 9 August 1855, Santa Anna, realizing a forced exile was imminent, departed Mexico City and was well on his way to Vera Cruz and exile before his intentions were discovered. First he went to Cuba and then to his estate in Colombia.[15]

The remaining twenty-one years of Santa Anna's life were occupied with exile, political intrigue, and unfulfilled schemes to return to power. Mexico may have been finished with Antonio López de Santa Anna, but he was not finished with Mexico. Foreigners found him an attractive alternative to those in power. On 18 March 1858, John Forsyth, the U.S. minister to Mexico, wrote to the Secretary of State: "I should have stronger hopes of making a favorable Treaty with Santa Anna than I have with the present Gov't. Santa Anna *will* have money, & he is not afraid to sell Territory if that be necessary to obtain it."[16]

The only remaining question for those opposed to Mexico's government was how to help Santa Anna engineer yet another comeback.

In early 1858, Santa Anna relocated from Colombia to the island of St. Thomas to be immediately available should he be recalled by one faction or another. And it was the Conservatives who flirted with Santa Anna, seeking his help in establishing a monarchy with a European prince. But Santa Anna was not inclined to be "second fiddle." Gambling on being able to tip things in his favor, Santa Anna returned to Vera Cruz on 28 February 1864. Before landing, he was required to sign not only a statement supporting Emperor Maximilian, the Austrian prince who had seized the government of Mexico with the help of Napoleon III, but also a pledge not to become active in politics. That same day, a proclamation appeared over Santa Anna's name stating that he had led the movement for democracy but now favored a constitutional monarchy. By no means provocative, this public statement nonetheless resulted in his enemies immediately seeing it as a violation of his agreement to abstain from politics, and he was immediately deported.[17]

Returning to St. Thomas, neither Santa Anna nor Emperor Maximilian was ready to completely sever their strained relations. Santa Anna persistently wrote advice, which included permitting his return, and Maximilian continued to pay Santa Anna's pension as a retired general of division but refused to authorize his return. Finally Santa Anna, accurately reading the death struggle of the Maximilian empire, chose to once again court the Liberals. Upon discovering this, Maximilian stopped Santa Anna's pension and confiscated his estate.

Santa Anna understood that whoever governed in Mexico in the future would be significantly influenced by the United States now that its Civil War was ending. He wrote to the United States seeking its support for his liberation of Mexico from the Europeans. Amazingly, no one less than Secretary of State William Seward, who was "vacationing" in St. Thomas, paid a "courtesy call" on Santa Anna. Santa Anna impressed the secretary as "a man of very good understanding, with very firm will and of good abilities as the leader of a party."[18]

Pathetically, the aging Santa Anna then fell victim to swindlers. A few people whom he employed as agents in the United States began telling the old dictator what he wanted to hear. Santa Anna then received a forged letter, supposedly from Secretary of State Seward, stating that the U.S. House of Representatives had approved a $50 million loan for Mexico, $30 million of which was earmarked for supporting Santa Anna's activities. Santa Anna rushed to New York where these con artists continued the ruse, fleecing the old man. After some months, when much of his fortune was gone, Santa Anna finally caught on.[19]

During his stay in New York, Santa Anna unknowingly altered American social habit. He employed one young James Adams as secretary and interpreter. The youth noticed that Santa Anna would slice a piece off a tropical plant and chew it. The general told him the plant was called *chicle* and on his departure gave the remainder to Adams. The enterprising man experimented by adding sweeteners to it, and within a few years he established the Adams Chewing Gum Company.[20]

Santa Anna had one more card to play in his quest for power. Using the last of his wealth, he decided to outfit a filibustering expedition, seize Vera Cruz, and declare a Conservative Republic. This plan had merit. Maximilian had been captured on 15 May 1867 and was condemned to death. Now the Mexican monarchists were leaderless, and other prominent Mexicans believed the Juárez government was too liberal.

Santa Anna's small expedition arrived off Vera Cruz on 3 June on board the U.S. merchant ship *Virginia*. An armed truce existed within the port. Many heavily armed pro-Maximilian supporters were prominent. Santa Anna announced that he was under the protection of the United States and wanted to address the officers of the port's garrison. They boarded the *Virginia* where the old dictator was unsuccessful in convincing them to join him.

Next, the ship was boarded by American Commander F. A. Roe, captain of the gunboat *Tacony*, and British Captain Charles Aynsley, commanding officer of the corvette *Jason*. Roe demanded to see proof that the old general was under American protection; this he could not produce since it did not exist. Appreciating that Santa Anna's landing was not in the best interest of American policy, Roe refused him entry. Santa Anna and Roe quickly came to heated words, and Roe told Santa Anna that he would have to spend the night on board the American warship, to which Santa Anna protested. When a compatriot of Santa Anna complained that Santa Anna was a cripple and that the threat of force was inappropriate, Roe responded that he "would take him [Santa Anna] if he had to break the other leg off the damned old scoundrel."[21]

The next day the *Virginia* picked up Santa Anna from the *Tacony*. The merchant ship sailed out of sight. During the next few days, Santa Anna unsuccessfully attempted to sneak ashore. Finally, the *Virginia* sailed for Sisal in the Yucatán. There Santa Anna sent ashore one of his typically flamboyant proclamations, this one stressing the need for peace, which Santa Anna would facilitate. He also posted a letter to his secret agent in Vera Cruz that revealed details of the recent failed landing at that port. This was intercepted and read by a local pro-Juárez official. A squad of Mexican soldiers boarded the *Virginia* and required Santa Anna to come ashore, where he was arrested. The Juárez government moved Santa Anna first to Campeche and then to Vera Cruz. Not sure of his fate, Santa Anna signed a new will and testament on 27 September 1867. In October Santa Anna was subjected to a court martial. The sentence was once again exile — undoubtedly the mildness of the verdict was influenced by the fact that he had been forcefully removed from an American merchant ship. On 1 November 1867, a British packet carried Santa Anna to Havana.[22]

Santa Anna was in Havana for a year when Spanish officials asked him to leave. He went to Puerto Plata and finally to Nassau. In 1870, when the Juárez government issued a general amnesty, Santa Anna was excluded. The old dictator continued to plot against the Liberal Juárez whom by now Santa Anna had elevated to his archenemy. His schemes became increasingly the ravings of an old, deluded, sick man.

Finally, Juárez died and the long-sought amnesty was granted. Santa Anna landed in Vera Cruz on 27 February 1874. He was met by a few old friends and took the new railroad to Mexico City where he arrived on 7 March. Santa Anna soon became embroiled in arguing with the government over money. The Mexican government, showing pity, talked in terms of a modest pension, whereas Santa Anna demanded full compensation for property and services, real and imagined. In the end, he received neither. He became increasingly depressed which was only relieved by his increasing senility. Santa Anna was suffering the worst possible punishment — obscurity and irrelevancy.

Antonio López de Santa Anna — eleven-times president of Mexico; general of division; grand master of the National and Distinguished Order of Guadalupe; knight commander of the Great Cross of the Royal and Distinguished Order of Charles III of Spain; holder of the Grand Cross of the Red Eagle of Prussia; and entitled by the Mexican Congress "Benefactor of the Nation" and "Most Serene Highness" — died on 21 June 1876, an old, impoverished, and broken man. There was one last hurrah — forty coaches followed his remains to their modest resting place in the Guadalupe Cemetery.[23]

Conservative patriarch and eminent historian Lucas Alamán wrote in the late 1840s concerning the early years of independence, "The history of Mexico that we are now entering might accurately be called the history of Santa Anna's revolutions...."[24]

Chapter 11

Conclusion

How could Antonio López de Santa Anna have dominated Mexico for so long? Two answers stand out above all others.

First, he was a political opportunist without equal. Santa Anna possessed no political principles and could not only easily adapt to the prevailing desire of the populace but also cleverly manipulate it. Liberal Lorenzo de Zavala wrote: "Since he [Santa Anna] has no fixed principles nor any organized code of public behavior, through his lack of understanding he always moves to extremes and comes to contradict himself. He does not measure his actions or calculate the results."[1]

Those who believed that they could control and exploit the popularity of Santa Anna, as did Gómez Frías and Lucas Alamán, the patriarchs of the political left and right, soon found themselves being the exploited.

Second, Santa Anna was most often victorious on the battlefield because of two qualities — he was audacious and brave. Typically, he traveled in advance of his army escorted by a few dragoons. This courting of danger inspired confidence in his soldiers.

Also, he ordered attacks without caring about the consequence of his actions upon his soldiers. His attacks against the Spanish at Tampico on 11 September 1829 and the Texans at the Alamo on 6 March 1836 are excellent examples. In both cases, these enemies were hopelessly trapped; he could have won each battle with considerably less loss of life to both sides by subjecting his enemies to a bombardment with his superior artillery. At the Alamo, one of his officers advised Santa Anna, "It [the assault] is going to cost many lives" and suggested that the general await the arrival of his heavy cannon. Santa Anna replied, "It is not important what it costs." [2]

Compounding the consequences of his brashness, Santa Anna did not want or accept advice from subordinates. General Vicente Filisola, Santa Anna's second in command during the 1836 Texas campaign, wrote: "Because of his [Santa Anna's] maxim of not subjecting military operations to discussion and confiding in his own inspiration which on other occasions had given him such happy results, His Excellency could not suffer an adverse criticism with patience." [3] Santa Anna himself confirmed this characteristic: "I am not in favor of discussions in councils of war to determine military operations." [4]

At first glance, claiming that Santa Anna was brave seems to contradict his actions following the Battle of San Jacinto. When under great stress from defeat, Santa Anna would on occasion panic briefly, then regain his composure. In 1826 Zavala wrote of Santa Anna, "The soul of the general cannot be contained by his body. . . . Defeat . . . maddens him . . . then he abandons himself to a feeling of weakness though not cowardice." [5]

When fighting against Mexican opponents, his bold, sometimes reckless, moves won out over his competitors' more timid decisions. Santa Anna and his Mexican rivals commanded feudal armies, which they raised and held together by patronage (from many of the officers) and coercion (toward most of the soldiers). In such an environment, the brave, risk-taking López de Santa Anna dominated. Only when he had to fight individuals leading armies of citizens (soldiers having a personal stake in the outcome) did Santa Anna's strategy for success — risk taking — prove disastrous; this was when his bravery proved not enough to overcome the enemy.

Friend and foe alike came to this conclusion. In 1848 fifteen Mexican officers wrote "Notes for the History of the War between Mexico and the United States." Their observations concerning Santa Anna at Buena Vista accurately capture the strengths and weaknesses of the eleven-time Mexican president: "Friends and enemies have recognized the valor with which he constantly braved the fire. It is to be regretted his combinations [tactics] did not correspond with his gallantry, that his errors dim the splendor of his merits, and that while it is painful to blame his conduct as a general, it is also pleasing to praise his courage as a soldier."[6]

American General Winfield Scott wrote, "His [Santa Anna's] vigilance and energy were unquestionable, and his powers of creating and organizing worthy of admiration. He was also great in administrative ability, and though not deficient in personal courage, he, on the field of battle, failed in quickness of perception and rapidity of combination. Hence his defeats."[7]

If Santa Anna was so well suited for his domestic political environment, what caused his demise? He may have been the most skilled political opportunist in Mexico, but he was not the only one. Zavala observed, "The evil of Mexico is not Santa Anna but the army. If Santa Anna were killed, the army will engender other Santa Annas."[8] On occasion, the selfish decisions of other *caudillos* contributed to Santa Anna's demise. Two battlefield examples of subordinates directly disobeying Santa Anna's orders were General Gabriel Valencia's decision on 19 August 1847 not to withdraw from Contreras, and General Juan Alvarez's decision on 8 September 1847 not to charge the American troops at Molino del Rey. These acts of insubordination contributed to the disastrous defeats that Santa Anna endured.

In addition, Santa Anna changed — he got old. Youth has significant advantages for a *caudillo*. By the 1860s, other bold young men had taken the political stage: for the political left, the youthful Porfirio Díaz and for the right, Miguel Miramón, each of whom would write their own chapters in Mexican history. Old age was the worst enemy of even the most talented *caudillo*.

And what was the curse of Antonio López de Santa Anna? By selling off Mexico's northern territories, which were rich in resources, he prevented Mexico for all time from developing into a world power. Juan O'Donoju, the last Spanish colonial administrator of Mexico, must have been a very insightful man. He barely knew revolutionary Colonel Antonio López de Santa Anna when in 1821 he prophesied, "This young man will live to make his country weep."[9]

Notes

Chapter 1

1. José Vasconcelos, *Breve historia de México* (Mexico: Editorial Polis, 1944), 428; Enrique Krauze, *Mexico Biography of Power* (New York: Harper Collins, 1997), 127, 141; Michael C. Meyer, William L. Sherman, and Susan M. Deeds, *The Course of Mexican History*, 6th ed. (New York: Oxford University Press, 1999), 320–21; Ruth R. Olivera and Liliane Crété, *Life in Mexico under Santa Anna, 1822–1855* (Norman, OK: University of Oklahoma Press, 1991), 123–24.

2. Meyer, Sherman, and Deeds, *Course of Mexican History*, 257; Ernest Gruening, *Mexico and Its Heritage* (New York: D. Appleton-Century, 1934), 290.

3. Jonathan Kandell, *La Capital: The Biography of Mexico City* (New York: Random House, 1988), 319; Leonardo Pasquel, *Antonio López de Santa Anna* (Mexico: Instituto de Mexicologia, 1990), 17–18.

4. Wilfrid Hardy Callcott, *Santa Anna* (Hamden, CT: Archon Books, 1964), 5–6; Kandell, *La Capital,* 320; Frank C. Hanighen, *Santa Anna: The Napoleon of the West* (New York: Coward-McCann, 1934), 7.

5. Hanighen, *Santa Anna,* 3–5; Antonio López de Santa Anna, *The Eagle: The Autobiography of Santa Anna,* ed. Ann Fears Crawford (Austin, TX: State House Press, 1988), 7–8; Callcott, *Santa Anna,* 10–11.

6. Callcott, *Santa Anna,* 12; Hanighen, *Santa Anna,* 5–6.

7. Hanighen, *Santa Anna,* 12–13.

8. Callcott, *Santa Anna,* 20–21; Hanighen, *Santa Anna,* 14–15; Thomas Ewing Cotner, *The Military and Political Career of José Joaquín De Herrera, 1792–1854* (New York: Greenwood Press, 1969), 36–37; Pasquel, *Antonio López de Santa Anna,* 25–26.

9. Cotner, *Military and Political Career,* 38.

10. Santa Anna, *The Eagle,* 9–12; William Spence Robertson, *Iturbide of Mexico* (Durham, NC: Duke University Press, 1952), 88–89.

11. Callcott, *Santa Anna,* 25–26.

12. Ibid., 30; Kandell, *La Capital,* 320.

13. Robertson, *Iturbide of Mexico,* 181; Callcott, *Santa Anna,* 34–35; José Bravo Ugarte, *Historia de México,* 3 vols. (Mexico: JUS, 1944), 3:134; Pasquel, *Antonio López de Santa Anna,* 30.

14. Alfonso Corona del Rosal, *La guerra, el imperialismo, el ejército mexicano* (Mexico: Grijalbo, 1989), 24.

15. Callcott, *Santa Anna,* 35, 38.

16. Hanighen, *Santa Anna,* 23; Pasquel, *Antonio López de Santa Anna,* 31–32.

Chapter 2

1. Cotner, *Military and Political Career,* 54; Callcott, *Santa Anna,* 38–39; Gruening, *Mexico and Its Heritage,* 47.

2. Hanighen, *Santa Anna,* 24–25.

3. Robertson, *Iturbide of Mexico,* 222.

4. Ibid., 223–24; Hanighen, *Santa Anna,* 25–26; Henry Bamford Parkes, *A History of Mexico* (Boston: Houghton Mifflin, 1938), 186; William A. DePalo, Jr., *The Mexican National Army, 1822–1852* (College Station, TX: Texas A & M University Press, 1997), 27–28.

5. Hubert Howe Bancroft, *History of Mexico,* 6 vols. (San Francisco: A. L. Bancroft, 1883–1886), 4:788–92; Meyer, Sherman, and Deeds, *Course of Mexican History,* 294–95; Pasquel, *Antonio López de Santa Anna,* 36–38; Gruening, *Mexico and Its Heritage,* 48.

6. Robertson, *Iturbide of Mexico,* 230–31; Gruening, *Mexico and Its Heritage,* 291; Lucas Alamán, *Historia de Méjico,* 5 vols. (Mexico: Libros del Bachiller Sansón Carrasco, 1986), 5:387–92; Bravo Ugarte, *Historia de México,* 3:150–54.

7. Callcott, *Santa Anna,* 49–51; Joseph H. L. Schlarman, *Mexico: A Land of Volcanoes* (Milwaukee, WI: Bruce, 1950), 237–38.

8. Hanighen, *Santa Anna,* 35.

9. Callcott, *Santa Anna,* 54–56; Pasquel, *Antonio López de Santa Anna,* 53.

10. Hanighen, *Santa Anna,* 43–44.

11. Meyer, Sherman, and Deeds, *Course of Mexican History,* 307.

12. Parkes, *A History of Mexico*, 193.

13. Hanighen, *Santa Anna*, 46–47.

14. Krauze, *Mexico*, 135; Hanighen, *Santa Anna*, 47–49.

15. Callcott, *Santa Anna*, 69; Krauze, *Mexico*, 135.

16. Meyer, Sherman, and Deeds, *Course of Mexican History*, 307.

17. Callcott, *Santa Anna*, 70–71.

18. Cotner, *Military and Political Career*, 300; Hanighen, *Santa Anna*, 49–50.

19. Meyer, Sherman, and Deeds, *Course of Mexican History*, 318–19; Callcott, *Santa Anna*, 58, 84, 188, 217.

Chapter 3

1. Callcott, *Santa Anna*, 73; Miguel A. Sánchez Lamego, "El ejército mexicano de 1821 a 1860," in *El ejército mexicano* (Mexico: Secretaría de la Defensa Nacional, 1979), 130–32; Bancroft, *History of Mexico* 5:71–73: Hanighen, *Santa Anna*, 51–52.

2. Bancroft, *History of Mexico*, 5:74; Callcott, *Santa Anna*, 71–74; Pasquel, *Antonio López de Santa Anna*, 54.

3. Callcott, *Santa Anna*, 74–75.

4. Krauze, *Mexico*, 135.

5. Sánchez Lamego, "El ejército mexicano," 135–36; Vasconcelos, *Breve historia de México*, 430; Guillermo Prieto, *Lecciones de historia patria*, 2 vols. (Mexico: Secretaría de la Defensa Nacional, 1996), 2:344–45; DePalo, *The Mexican National Army*, 38–39; Hanighen, *Santa Anna*, 59–61.

6. Callcott, *Santa Anna*, 85–87; Hanighen, *Santa Anna*, 62–63.

7. Henry Tudor, *Narrative of a Tour in North America*, 2 vols. (London: James Duncan Paternoster Row, 1834), 2:164–65; Hanighen, *Santa Anna*, 64–65; Bravo Ugarte, *Historia de México*, 3:179–80.

8. Callcott, *Santa Anna*, 90–91; Hanighen, *Santa Anna*, 18; Pasquel, *Antonio López de Santa Anna*, 61.

9. Hanighen, *Santa Anna*, 66–67.

10. Cotner, *Military and Political Career*, 76; Parkes, *A History of Mexico*, 195–96.

11. Callcott, *Santa Anna*, 92–95; Hanighen, *Santa Anna*, 67–68; Cotner, *Military and Political Career*, 77; Margaret Swett Henson, *Lorenzo de Zavala: The Pragmatic Idealist* (Fort Worth: Texas Christian University Press, 1996), 59.

Chapter 4

1. Meyer, Sherman, and Deeds, *Course of Mexican History,* 309–10.
2. Krauze, *Mexico,* 137; Hanighen, *Santa Anna,* 71–72; Callcott, *Santa Anna,* 97–106.
3. Meyer, Sherman, and Deeds, *Course of Mexican History,* 314–15; Parkes, *A History of Mexico,* 196–97; Olivera and Crété, *Life in Mexico,* 9.
4. Cotner, *Military and Political Career,* 77–78; Hanighen, *Santa Anna,* 73–75; Krauze, *Mexico,* 137; Bravo Ugarte, *Historia de México,* 3:180–81.
5. Gruening, *Mexico and Its Heritage,* 197–98; Parkes, *A History of Mexico,* 197.
6. Henson, *Lorenzo de Zavala,* 76; DePalo, *The Mexican National Army,* 44; Hanighen, *Santa Anna,* 77–78.
7. Callcott, *Santa Anna,* 115–16; Pedro Santoni, *Mexicans at Arms* (Fort Worth, TX: Texas Christian University Press, 1996), 18–19.
8. Callcott, *Santa Anna,* 124–25.
9. Robert A. Calvert and Arnold De León, *The History of Texas* (Arlington Heights, TX: Harlan Davidson, 1990), 56; DePalo, *The Mexican National Army,* 48–49.
10. Vasconcelos, *Breve historia de México,* 434.
11. Hanighen, *Santa Anna,* 81–82.
12. DePalo, *The Mexican National Army,* 52.
13. Hanighen, *Santa Anna,* 82.
14. Carlos E. Castañeda, *The Mexican Side of the Texas Revolution* (Washington, DC: Documentary Publications, 1971), 100.
15. Callcott, *Santa Anna,* 127–28; Vasconcelos, *Breve historia de México,* 434–36; Hanighen, *Santa Anna,* 82–83; Parkes, *A History of Mexico,* 202–03.
16. Philip Haythornthwaite, *The Alamo and the War of Texas Independence, 1835–36* (London: Osprey, 1986), 22; Calvert and De León, *The History of Texas,* 68–69; Bill Groneman, *Battlefields of Texas* (Plano, TX: Republic of Texas Press, 1998), 48–52; Terry Hooker, *The Revolt in Texas Leading to Its Independence from Mexico, 1835–36* (Cottingham, England: El Dorado Books, 1993), 39.
17. Krauze, *Mexico,* 139; Hanighen, *Santa Anna,* 89–90.
18. Callcott, *Santa Anna,* 131; Hanighen, *Santa Anna,* 87; Vasconcelos, *Breve historia de México,* 437.

Chapter 5

1. Callcott, *Santa Anna,* 129–33.
2. Castañeda, *Mexican Side of the Texas Revolution,* 15, 171; DePalo, *The Mexican National Army,* 59; Hanighen, *Santa Anna,* 100.
3. Castañeda, *Mexican Side of the Texas Revolution,* 216–29; Vasconcelos, *Breve historia de México,* 438; Calvert and De León, *The History of Texas,* 69–70; Meyer, Sherman, and Deeds, *Course of Mexican History,* 328–29.
4. Castañeda, *Mexican Side of the Texas Revolution,* 20.
5. Vasconcelos, *Breve historia de México,* 441; Hanighen, *Santa Anna,* 108–09.
6. Henson, *Lorenzo de Zavala,* 106–07; Callcott, *Santa Anna,* 134; Vasconcelos, *Breve historia de México,* 439–40; Parkes, *A History of Mexico,* 204.
7. Calvert and De León, *The History of Texas,* 70; Haythornthwaite, *Alamo and War of Texas Independence,* 22; Groneman, *Battlefields of Texas,* 67–71; Castañeda, *Mexican Side of the Texas Revolution,* 31–32; DePalo, *The Mexican National Army,* 62.
8. Ralph E. Dittman, "Santa Anna's Battle of New Orleans," *Louisiana History* 25 (1984): 189–90; Vasconcelos, *Breve historia de México,* 442–43; Herbert Priestley, *The Mexican Nation: A History* (New York: Macmillan, 1935), 284–85; Callcott, *Santa Anna,* 137.
9. Hanighen, *Santa Anna,* 78; Callcott, *Santa Anna,* 137–39.
10. Castañeda, *Mexican Side of the Texas Revolution,* 40.
11. Callcott, *Santa Anna,* 139; Hanighen, *Santa Anna,* 116–18.
12. Andrew Jackson, *Correspondence of Andrew Jackson,* 7 vols., ed. John Spencer Bassett (Washington, DC: Carnegie Institution of Washington, 1929–37), 5:425; Meyer, Sherman, and Deeds, *Course of Mexican History,* 328; Callcott, *Santa Anna,* 141–42.
13. Callcott, *Santa Anna,* 145; Vasconcelos, *Breve historia de México,* 447.
14. Callcott, *Santa Anna,* 147–48; Henson, *Lorenzo de Zavala,* 111–13.
15. Callcott, *Santa Anna,* 149–52; Hanighen, *Santa Anna,* 140–41.
16. Santa Anna, *The Eagle,* 54–55.
17. Santa Anna, *The Eagle,* 53.

Chapter 6

1. Callcott, *Santa Anna,* 154–55; Hanighen, *Santa Anna,* 144.
2. Antonio de la Peña y Reyes, *La primera guerra entre México y*

Francia (México: Publicaciones de la Secretaría de Relaciones Exteriores, 1927), 120–41; Nancy Nichols Baker, *The French Experience in Mexico, 1821–1861* (Chapel Hill: University of North Carolina Press, 1979), 73–75.

3. A. du Sein, *Histoire de la marine de tous les peuples depuis les temps les plus reculés jusqu'à nos jours,* 2 vols. (Paris: Fuimin Didot Frères, 1863), 2:691–93; André Reussner and Louis Nicolas, *La puissance navale dans l'histoire,* 3 vols. (Paris: Éditions Maritimes et Coloniales, 1958–63), 2:26; Joannès Tramond and André Reussner, *Éléments d'histoire maritime et coloniale, 1815–1914* (Paris: Société d'Éditions Géographiques Maritimes et Coloniales, 1924), 29; René Jouan, *Histoire de la marine française* (Paris: Payot, 1932), 215–16; DePalo, *The Mexican National Army,* 68–69; Eugène Maissin, *The French in Mexico and Texas (1838–1839),* trans. James L. Shepard III (Solado, TX: Anson Jones Press, 1961), 52; Meyer, Sherman, and Deeds, *Course of Mexican History,* 315–16; Callcott, *Santa Anna,* 157; Hanighen, *Santa Anna,* 148–49.

4. Hanighen, *Santa Anna,* 149–50.

5. Callcott, *Santa Anna,* 157; Hanighen, *Santa Anna,* 150.

6. Hanighen, *Santa Anna,* 150–51.

7. Callcott, *Santa Anna,* 158–59; Hanighen, *Santa Anna,* 152–53; Krauze, *Mexico,* 140.

8. Callcott, *Santa Anna,* 159; Hanighen, *Santa Anna,* 153–55.

9. Callcott, *Santa Anna,* 160; Olivera and Crété, *Life in Mexico,* 13; Hanighen, *Santa Anna,* 156–57.

10. Callcott, *Santa Anna,* 161.

11. Hanighen, *Santa Anna,* 157.

12. DePalo, *The Mexican National Army,* 71–72; Callcott, *Santa Anna,* 162–63.

13. Hanighen, *Santa Anna,* 157–58; Pasquel, *Antonio López de Santa Anna,* 89.

14. Callcott, *Santa Anna,* 169.

15. DePalo, *The Mexican National Army,* 77–78; Cotner, *Military and Political Career,* 98–99; Callcott, *Santa Anna,* 172–74.

16. Miguel A. Sánchez Lamego, *The Second Mexican-Texas War, 1841–1843* (Hillsboro, TX: A. Hill Junior College Monograph, 1972), 75–84; George L. Rives, *The United States and Mexico,* 2 vols. (New York: Charles A. Scribner's Sons, 1913), 1:485; DePalo, *The Mexican National Army,* 82–83; Calvert and De León, *The History of Texas,* 91.

17. Sánchez Lamego, *Second Mexican-Texas War,* 89–91.
18. Ibid.
19. DePalo, *The Mexican National Army,* 83–84.
20. Callcott, *Santa Anna,* 181; Hanighen, *Santa Anna,* 176–77.
21. Callcott, *Santa Anna,* 183, 200–04; Castañeda, *Mexican Side of the Texas Revolution,* 110–11; Krauze, *Mexico,* 141.
22. Hanighen, *Santa Anna,* 177–78.
23. Pasquel, *Antonio López de Santa Anna,* 100; Cotner, *Military and Political Career,* 102–03.
24. Callcott, *Santa Anna,* 206–08; Cotner, *Military and Political Career,* 104–05; DePalo, *The Mexican National Army,* 86–87; Hanighen, *Santa Anna,* 186–87.
25. Manuel Rivera Cambas, *Los Gobernantes de México,* 2 vols. (Mexico: Imp. De J. M. Agular Ortiz, 1873), 2:282; Cotner, *Military and Political Career,* 118.
26. DePalo, *The Mexican National Army,* 87; Bravo Ugarte, *Historia de México,* 3:195–96; Priestley, *The Mexican Nation,* 297–98; Hanighen, *Santa Anna,* 187–90.
27. Cotner, *Military and Political Career,* 114–15.
28. Callcott, *Santa Anna,* 219; Hanighen, *Santa Anna,* 190–91.

Chapter 7

1. Krauze, *Mexico,* 141; Callcott, *Santa Anna,* 223–25; Gruening, *Mexico and Its Heritage,* 252; Hanighen, *Santa Anna,* 191–93.
2. C. Alan Hutchinson, "Valentín Gómez Farías and the Movement for the Return of General Santa Anna to Mexico in 1846," in *Essays in Mexican History,* ed. Thomas Cotner (Austin, TX: University of Texas Press, 1958), 183; Santoni, *Mexicans at Arms,* 114–15.
3. Santoni, *Mexicans at Arms,* 15–16; Hanighen, *Santa Anna,* 196.
4. Hutchinson, "Valentín Gómez Farías," 183–84; Jack K. Bauer, *The Mexican War, 1846–1848* (New York: Macmillan, 1974), 27–28; Hanighen, *Santa Anna,* 196.
5. Bauer, *The Mexican War,* 76–77; Hanighen, *Santa Anna,* 197–99.
6. Hanighen, *Santa Anna,* 203–04.
7. Richard Hitchman, "Rush to Glory," *Strategy and Tactics* 127 (June–July 1989): 21; DePalo, *The Mexican National Army,* 108; Bancroft, *History of Mexico,* 5:301–03.
8. Bauer, *The Mexican War,* 89–90.
9. Manuel Balbontín, *La invasión americana, 1846 a 1848* (Mexico:

Tip. De Gonzalo A. Esteva, 1883), 49–50; José María Roa Bárcena, *Recuerdos de la invasión norteamericana (1846–1848),* 3 vols. (Mexico: Editorial Porrua, S. A., 1971), 1:122; Ramón Alcaraz, *The Other Side, or Notes for the History of the War between Mexico and the United States,* ed. Albert C. Ramsey (New York: Burt Franklin, 1850), 79–80.

10. James Polk, *Polk: The Diary of a President, 1845–1849,* ed. Allan Nevins (New York: Longmans, Green, 1952), 154–59, 164–65.

11. Hanighen, *Santa Anna,* 203–07; Bauer, *The Mexican War,* 201.

12 Balbontín, *La invasión americana,* 55; Alcaraz, *The Other Side,* 83–85; Roa Bárcena, *Recuerdos de la invasión norteamericana,* 1:126–27; Olivera and Crété, *Life in Mexico,* 162.

13. Balbontín, *La invasión americana,* 56.

14. Hanighen, *Santa Anna,* 205.

15. Schlarman, *Mexico: A Land of Volcanoes,* 283; Guillermo Canales Montejano, *Historia Militar de México* (Mexico: Ediciones Ateneo, 1940), 91–92; Bravo Ugarte, *Historia de México,* 3:200; Balbontín, *La invasión americana,* 58–60.

16. Bauer, *The Mexican War,* 201–02; Balbontín, *La invasión americana,* 54.

17. Justin H. Smith, ed., "Letters of General Antonio López de Santa Anna Relating to the War between the United States and Mexico, 1846–48," *Annual Report of the American Historical Association for the Year 1917,* 2 vols. (Washington, DC: Government Printing Office, 1920), 2:368–71, 378–79.

18. Hanighen, *Santa Anna,* 206.

19. Bauer, *The Mexican War,* 204–05.

20. Canales Montejano, *Historia Militar de México,* 89, 95.

21. Ellen Hardin Walworth, "The Battle of Buena Vista," *Magazine of American History* (New York: A. S. Barbes, 1879), 3, part 2, 717–18.

22. Bauer, *The Mexican War,* 206; Roa Bárcena, *Recuerdos de la invasión norteamericana,* 1:199–201; Balbontín, *La invasión americana,* 60–61; Alcaraz, *The Other Side,* 98.

23. Olivera and Crété, *Life in Mexico,* 162; Bauer, *The Mexican War,* 208–09.

24. Balbontín, *La invasión americana,* 71; Parkes, *A History of Mexico,* 216; Canales Montejano, *Historia Militar de México,* 97–98.

25. Walworth, "The Battle of Buena Vista," 718; Balbontín, *La invasión americana,* 70.

26. Balbontín, *La invasión americana,* 70–71.

27. Bauer, *The Mexican War,* 208–09; Canales Montejano, *Historia Militar de México,* 97.

28. Bauer, *The Mexican War,* 209–10; Balbontín, *La invasión americana,* 74; Canales Montejano, *Historia Militar de México,* 98–99.

29. Balbontín, *La invasión americana,* 72–73.

30. Walworth, "The Battle of Buena Vista," 721; Bauer, *The Mexican War,* 210–11.

31. Bauer, *The Mexican War,* 211; Canales Montejano, *Historia Militar de México,* 99; DePalo, *The Mexican National Army,* 110–11.

32. Walworth, "The Battle of Buena Vista," 727–29; Parkes, *A History of Mexico,* 216; Canales Montejano, *Historia Militar de México,* 100–01; Balbontín, *La invasión americana,* 72–73, 80–81.

33. Bauer, *The Mexican War,* 214.

34. Bauer, *The Mexican War,* 215; Walworth, "The Battle of Buena Vista," 729–30.

35. Bauer, *The Mexican War,* 215–16.

36. Olivera and Crété, *Life in Mexico,* 165; Walworth, "The Battle of Buena Vista," 733–35; Balbontín, *La invasión americana,* 84–85; Hanighen, *Santa Anna,* 213–14.

37. Walworth, "The Battle of Buena Vista," 736.

38. Walworth, "The Battle of Buena Vista," 735–36; Bauer, *The Mexican War,* 215–16.

39. Canales Montejano, *Historia Militar de México,* 102–03; Bauer, *The Mexican War,* 216; DePalo, *The Mexican National Army,* 111–13.

40. Canales Montejano, *Historia Militar de México,* 102; Olivera and Crété, *Life in Mexico,* 165; Roa Bárcena, *Recuerdos de la invasión norteamericana,* 1:166–74, 185. Flags were very important symbols on nineteenth-century battlefields, and their capture carried special significance. During the U.S Civil War, many Congressional Medals of Honor were awarded for capturing Confederate flags.

41. Alcaraz, *The Other Side,* 137.

42. Ibid., 137–41; *The Mexican Soldier* (Mexico: Nieto-Brown-Hefter, 1958), 77–78; Canales Montejano, *Historia Militar de México,* 103–04; Olivera and Crété, *Life in Mexico,* 15.

43. Canales Montejano, *Historia Militar de México,* 107–08; Balbontín, *La invasión americana,* 90–101; Vasconcelos, *Breve historia de México,* 455; Hanighen, *Santa Anna,* 214–16.

44. Hanighen, *Santa Anna,* 216.

Chapter 8

1. DePalo, *The Mexican National Army,* 115; Balbontín, *La invasión americana,* 103–04; Roa Bárcena, *Recuerdos de la invasión norteamericana,* 1:245–48.
2. Balbontín, *La invasión americana,* 104–05.
3. Bravo Ugarte, *Historia de México,* 3:200–01; Hanighen, *Santa Anna,* 216–18; Callcott, *Santa Anna,* 255–57; DePalo, *The Mexican National Army,* 115–16.
4. Bauer, *The Mexican War,* 260–64.
5. Hitchman, "Rush to Glory," 21–22.
6. DePalo, *The Mexican National Army,* 120–21; Bauer, *The Mexican War,* 263–64; Callcott, *Santa Anna,* 259–60.
7. Hanighen, *Santa Anna,* 222.
8. Smith, "Letters of Santa Anna," 2:347; Roa Bárcena, *Recuerdos de la invasión norteamericana,* 2:16–17.
9. Bauer, *The Mexican War,* 264–65; DePalo, *The Mexican National Army,* 123; Hanighen, *Santa Anna,* 222–23.
10. DePalo, *The Mexican National Army,* 123–24; Roa Bárcena, *Recuerdos de la invasión norteamericana,* 2:23–48; Bauer, *The Mexican War,* 267–68; Hanighen, *Santa Anna,* 224.
11. DePalo, *The Mexican National Army,* 124.
12. Pasquel, *Antonio López de Santa Anna,* 128.
13. José Fernando Ramírez, *Mexico during the War with the United States,* ed. Walter V. Scholes (Columbia: University of Missouri, 1950), 120.

Chapter 9

1. Meyer, Sherman, and Deeds, *Course of Mexican History,* 337; Bauer, *The Mexican War,* 271–72; Hanighen, *Santa Anna,* 226.
2. Ramírez, *Mexico during the War,* 120.
3. Ramírez, *Mexico during the War,* 134.
4. Hanighen, *Santa Anna,* 227–28.
5. Callcott, *Santa Anna,* 265; G. P. Stokes, "War with Mexico," *Command Military History, Strategy & Analysis* 40 (November 1996): 43; Bauer, *The Mexican War,* 287–88.
6. DePalo, *The Mexican National Army,* 126–27; Stokes, "War with Mexico," 43; Bauer, *The Mexican War,* 286–87.
7. Carlos E. Castañeda, "Relations of General Scott with Santa Anna," *Hispanic American Historical Review* 29 (November 1949): 461.

8. Ibid., 465–66.

9. Rives, *The United States and Mexico,* 2:445–46; Ethan Allen Hitchcock, *Fifty Years in Camp and Field* (New York: G. P. Putnam's Sons, 1909), 268–69.

10. Castañeda, "Relations of General Scott," 468–69.

11. DePalo, *The Mexican National Army,* 126–27; Alcaraz, *The Other Side,* 261; Roa Bárcena, *Recuerdos de la invasión norteamericana,* 2:175–83; Balbontín, *La invasión americana,* 108–09.

12. Winfield Scott, *Memoirs of Lieut. General Scott, LL.D.* (New York: Sheldon, 1864), 467–68; Smith, "Letters of Santa Anna," 2:372–73; Thaddeus Holt, "Checkmate at Mexico City," *Quarterly Journal of Military History* 2 (spring 1990): 84.

13. DePalo, *The Mexican National Army,* 128–29; Balbontín, *La invasión americana,* 114–16; Bauer, *The Mexican War,* 291–95; Holt, "Checkmate at Mexico City," 89–90.

14. Bauer, *The Mexican War,* 295–96; Balbontín, *La invasión americana,* 116–18; Roa Bárcena, *Recuerdos de la invasión norteamericana,* 2:220–28, 241–42; Hanighen, *Santa Anna,* 232–35.

15. *The Mexican Soldier,* 78; Hitchman, "Rush to Glory," 26; Bauer, *The Mexican War,* 295–96.

16. Hitchman, "Rush to Glory," 26; Bauer, *The Mexican War,* 299–300; Holt, "Checkmate at Mexico City," 91–92.

17. *The Mexican Soldier,* 54; Ramírez, *Mexico during the War,* 152; Bauer, *The Mexican War,* 301; Balbontín, *La invasión americana,* 119–23.

18. Castañeda, "Relations of General Scott," 457; Santoni, *Mexicans at Arms,* 211; Holt, "Checkmate at Mexico City," 93.

19. DePalo, *The Mexican National Army,* 132–33; Holt, "Checkmate at Mexico City," 85; Bauer, *The Mexican War,* 306–07.

20. Bauer, *The Mexican War,* 307–08; Cotner, *Military and Political Career,* 162–63.

21. Balbontín, *La invasión americana,* 126–29; Hanighen, *Santa Anna,* 236; Pasquel, *Antonio López de Santa Anna,* 132.

22. DePalo, *The Mexican National Army,* 133–35; Alcaraz, *The Other Side,* 339–43; Bauer, *The Mexican War,* 308–12.

23. Stokes, "War with Mexico," 48–49; Alcaraz, *The Other Side,* 356–57; DePalo, *The Mexican National Army,* 135–37.

24. Hitchman, "Rush to Glory," 26; Balbontín, *La invasión americana,* 130–32; DePalo, *The Mexican National Army,* 137–38; Bauer, *The Mexican War,* 312–18.

25. Pasquel, *Antonio López de Santa Anna*, 132.

26. DePalo, *The Mexican National Army*, 138–40; Stokes, "War with Mexico," 50–51; Balbontín, *La invasión americana*, 123; Smith, "Letters of Santa Anna," 2:415–16.

27. Hanighen, *Santa Anna*, 240–42; Callcott, *Santa Anna*, 270–72; Bauer, *The Mexican War*, 331–32; Pasquel, *Antonio López de Santa Anna*, 136.

28. Hanighen, *Santa Anna*, 245–49; Callcott, *Santa Anna*, 272–76; Vasconcelos, *Breve historia de México*, 460; Parkes, *A History of Mexico*, 221.

29. Bauer, *The Mexican War*, 332.

30. DePalo, *The Mexican National Army*, 131.

31. Ibid., 114.

32. Ibid., 139; Hitchman, "Rush to Glory," 16.

33. Hitchman, "Rush to Glory," 14.

34. Callcott, *Santa Anna*, 262–63; Bauer, *The Mexican War*, 284–85.

35. Cotner, *Military and Political Career*, 169.

Chapter 10

1. Callcott, *Santa Anna*, 278–79.

2. Ibid., 272; Hanighen, *Santa Anna*, 260–61; Pasquel, *Antonio López de Santa Anna*, 147; Parkes, *A History of Mexico*, 225.

3. Gruening, *Mexico and Its Heritage*, 200.

4. Olivera and Crété, *Life in Mexico*, 15–16; Callcott, *Santa Anna*, 281–88; Krauze, *Mexico*, 148.

5. Gruening, *Mexico and Its Heritage*, 200–201; Krauze, *Mexico*, 167; Callcott, *Santa Anna*, 286–94; Hanighen, *Santa Anna*, 282.

6. Hanighen, *Santa Anna*, 269–70.

7. Hubert Howe Bancroft, *History of the Northern Mexican States*, 2 vols. (San Francisco: History Company, 1889), 2:684–86; Rives, *The United States and Mexico*, 2:169.

8. Bancroft, *History of the Northern Mexican States*, 2:686–92; W. O. Scroggs, *Filibusters and Financiers* (New York: Macmillan, 1916), 54; Rives, *The United States and Mexico*, 2:169–70.

9. Callcott, *Santa Anna*, 301.

10. Hanighen, *Santa Anna*, 281.

11. Vasconcelos, *Breve historia de México*, 468–70; Lilia Díaz, "El liberalismo militante," in *Historia general de México*, 2 vols. (Mexico: HARLA [Harper and Row Latinoamericana], 1988), 2:830;

Hanighen, *Santa Anna*, 280; Bravo Ugarte, *Historia de México*, 3:216.

12. Santa Anna, *The Eagle*, 144–45.

13. Callcott, *Santa Anna*, 307–08; Hanighen, *Santa Anna*, 279.

14. Parkes, *A History of Mexico*, 226–27; Callcott, *Santa Anna*, 308–09.

15. Hanighen, *Santa Anna*, 282–83; Díaz, "El liberalismo militante," 2:831; Parkes, *A History of Mexico*, 228–29; Callcott, *Santa Anna*, 312–15.

16. Callcott, *Santa Anna*, 323–24.

17. Callcott, *Santa Anna*, 325–31; Hanighen, *Santa Anna*, 293–94.

18. Callcott, *Santa Anna*, 338; Hanighen, *Santa Anna*, 296–97.

19. Callcott, *Santa Anna*, 339–44; Parkes, *A History of Mexico*, 229; Hanighen, *Santa Anna*, 295–96.

20. Hanighen, *Santa Anna*, 298.

21. Hanighen, *Santa Anna*, 300–01; Callcott, *Santa Anna*, 345.

22. Callcott, *Santa Anna*, 346–50.

23. Hanighen, *Santa Anna*, 305–06; Callcott, *Santa Anna*, 351–55; DePalo, *The Mexican National Army*, 38; Pasquel, *Antonio López de Santa Anna*, 175.

24. Alamán, *Historia de Méjico*, 5:396.

Chapter 11

1. Krauze, *Mexico*, 137.

2. Vasconcelos, *Breve historia de México*, 437; Callcott, *Santa Anna*, 102; Krauze, *Mexico*, 135; Prieto, *Lecciones de historia patria*, 2:237.

3. Castañeda, *Mexican Side of the Texas Revolution*, 172.

4. Ibid., 26.

5. Krauze, *Mexico*, 137.

6. Alcaraz, *The Other Side*, 129.

7. Scott, *Memoirs of Lieut. General Scott*, 466.

8. Vasconcelos, *Breve historia de México*, 429.

9. Santa Anna, *The Eagle*, 257.

Selected Bibliography

Alamán, Lucas. *Historia de Méjico.* 5 vols. Mexico: Libros del Bachiller Sansón Carrasco, 1986.

Alcaraz, Ramón. *The Other Side, or Notes for the History of the War between Mexico and the United States.* Edited by Albert C. Ramsey. New York: Burt Franklin, 1850.

Baker, Nancy Nichols. *The French Experience in Mexico, 1821–1861.* Chapel Hill: University of North Carolina Press, 1979.

Balbontín, Manuel. *La invasión americana 1846 a 1848.* Mexico: Tip. De Gonzalo A. Esteva, 1883.

Bancroft, Hubert Howe. *History of Mexico.* 6 vols. San Francisco: A. L. Bancroft, 1883–86.

Bancroft, Hubert Howe. *History of the Northern Mexican States.* 2 vols. San Francisco: History Company, 1889.

Bauer, Jack K. *The Mexican War 1846–1848.* New York: Macmillan, 1974.

Bravo Ugarte, José. *Historia de México.* 3 vols. Mexico: JUS, 1944.

Callcott, Wilfrid Hardy. *Santa Anna.* Hamden, CT: Archon Books, 1964.

Calvert, Robert A. and Arnold de León. *The History of Texas.* Arlington Heights, TX: Harlan Davidson, 1990.

Canales Montejano, Guillermo. *Historia Militar de México.* Mexico: Ediciones Ateneo, 1940.

Castañeda, Carlos E. *The Mexican Side of the Texas Revolution.* Washington, DC: Documentary Publications, 1971.

Castañeda, Carlos E. "Relations of General Scott with Santa Anna." *Hispanic American Historical Review* 29 (November 1949): 4, 455–73.

Corona del Rosal, Alfonso. *La guerra, el imperialismo, el ejército mexicano.* Mexico: Grijalbo, 1989.

Cotner, Thomas Ewing. *The Military and Political Career of José Joaquín De Herrera, 1792–1854.* New York: Greenwood Press, 1969.

DePalo, Jr., William A. *The Mexican National Army, 1822–1852.* College Station: Texas A & M University Press, 1997.

Díaz, Lilia. "El liberalismo militante." In *Historia general de México.* 2 vols. Mexico: HARLA [Harper and Row Latinoamericana], 1988.

Dittman, Ralph E. "Santa Anna's Battle of New Orleans." *Louisiana History* 25 (1984): 189–97.

Groneman, Bill. *Battlefields of Texas.* Plano, TX: Republic of Texas Press, 1998.

Gruening, Ernest. *Mexico and Its Heritage.* New York: D. Appleton-Century, 1934.

Hanighen, Frank C. *Santa Anna: The Napoleon of the West.* New York: Coward-McCann, 1934.

Haythornthwaite, Philip. *The Alamo and the War of Texas Independence, 1835–36.* London: Osprey, 1986.

Henson, Margaret Swett. *Lorenzo de Zavala: The Pragmatic Idealist.* Fort Worth: Texas Christian University Press, 1996.

Hitchcock, Ethan Allen. *Fifty Years in Camp and Field.* New York: G. P. Putnam's Sons, 1909.

Hitchman, Richard. "Rush to Glory." *Strategy and Tactics* 127 (June–July 1989): 14–26, 60, 62.

Holt, Thaddeus. "Checkmate at Mexico City." *Quarterly Journal of Military History* 2 (spring 1990): 3, 82–93.

Hooker, Terry. *The Revolt in Texas Leading to Its Independence from Mexico 1835–1836.* Cottingham, England: El Dorado Books, 1993.

Hutchinson, C. Alan. "Valentín Gómez Farías and the Movement for the Return of General Santa Anna to Mexico in 1846." In *Essays in Mexican History,* edited by Thomas Cotner. Austin: University of Texas Press, 1958.

Jackson, Andrew. *Correspondence of Andrew Jackson.* 7 vols. Edited by John Spencer Bassett. Washington, DC: Carnegie Institution of Washington, 1929–37.

Jouan, René. *Histoire de la marine française.* Paris: Payot, 1932.

Kandell, Jonathan. *La Capital: The Biography of Mexico City.* New York: Random House, 1988.

Krauze, Enrique. *Mexico Biography of Power.* New York: HarperCollins, 1997.

Maissin, Eugène. *The French in Mexico and Texas, (1838–1839).* Translated by James L. Shepherd III. Solado, TX: Anson Jones Press, 1961.

Meyer, Michael C., William L. Sherman, and Susan M. Deeds. *The Course of Mexican History.* 6th ed. New York: Oxford University Press, 1999.

The Mexican Soldier. Mexico: Nieto-Brown-Hefter, 1958.

Olivera, Ruth R. and Liliane Crété. *Life in Mexico under Santa Anna, 1822–1855.* Norman: University of Oklahoma Press, 1991.

Parkes, Henry Bamford. *A History of Mexico.* Boston: Houghton Mifflin, 1938.

Pasquel, Leonardo. *Antonio López de Santa Anna.* Mexico: Instituto de Mexicologia, 1990.

Peña y Reyes, Antonio de la. *La primera guerra entre México y Francia.* México: Publicaciones de la Secretaría de Relaciones Exteriores, 1927.

Polk, James. *Polk: The Diary of a President, 1845–1849.* Edited by Allan Nevins. New York: Longmans, Green, 1952.

Priestley, Herbert. *The Mexican Nation: A History.* New York: Macmillan, 1935.

Prieto, Guillermo. *Lecciones de historia patria.* 2 vols. Mexico: Secretaría de la Defensa Nacional, 1996.

Prieto, Guillermo. *Memorias de mis tiempos.* 2 vols. Paris: Vda. de C. Bouret, 1906.

Ramírez, José Fernando. *Mexico during the War with the United States.* Edited by Walter V. Scholes. Columbia: University of Missouri, 1950.

Reussner, André, and Louis Nicolas. *La puissance navale dans l'histoire.* 3 vols. Paris: Éditions Maritimes et Coloniales, 1958–63.

Rivera Cambas, Manuel. *Los gobernantes de México.* 2 vols. Mexico: Imp. de J. M. Agular Ortiz, 1873.

Rives, George L. *The United States and Mexico.* 2 vols. New York: Charles A. Scribner's Sons, 1913.

Roa Bárcena, José María. *Recuerdos de la invasión norteamericana (1846–1848).* 3 vols. Mexico: Editorial Porrua, S. A., 1971.

Robertson, William Spence. *Iturbide of Mexico.* Durham, NC: Duke University Press, 1952.

Sánchez Lamego, Miguel A. "El ejército mexicano de 1821 a 1860." In *El ejército mexicano.* Mexico: Secretaría de la Defensa Nacional, 1979.

Sánchez Lamego, Miguel A. *The Second Mexican-Texas War, 1841–1843.* Hillsboro, TX: A. Hill Junior College Monograph, 1972.

Santa Anna, Antonio López de. *The Eagle: The Autobiography of Santa Anna.* Edited by Ann Fears Crawford. Austin, TX: State House Press, 1988.

Santoni, Pedro. *Mexicans at Arms.* Fort Worth: Texas Christian University Press, 1996.

Schlarman, Joseph H. L. *Mexico: A Land of Volcanoes.* Milwaukee, WI: Bruce, 1950.

Scott, Winfield. *Memoirs of Lieut.-General Scott, LL.D.* New York: Sheldon, 1864.

Scroggs, W. O. *Filibusters and Financiers.* New York: Macmillan, 1916.

Sein, A. du. *Histoire de la marine de tous les peuples depuis les temps les plus reculés jusqu'à nos jours.* 2 vols. Paris: Fuimin Didot Frères, 1863.

Smith, Justin H., ed. "Letters of General Antonio Lopez de Santa Anna relating to the War between the United States and Mexico, 1846–48." *Annual Report of the American Historical Association for the Year 1917.* Washington, DC: Government Printing Office, 1920.

Smith, Justin H. *The War with Mexico.* New York: Macmillan, 1919.

Stokes, G. P. "War with Mexico." *Command Military History, Strategy & Analysis* 40 (November 1996): 34–51.

Tramond, Joannès and André Reussner. *Éléments d'histoire maritime et coloniale, 1815–1914.* Paris: Société d'Éditions Géographiques Maritimes et Coloniales, 1924.

Tudor, Henry. *Narrative of a Tour in North America.* 2 vols. London: James Duncan Paternoster Row, 1834.

Vasconcelos, José. *Breve historia de México.* Mexico: Editorial Polis, 1944.

Walworth, Ellen Hardin. "The Battle of Buena Vista." *Magazine of American History.* Vol. 3, part 2. New York: A. S. Barbes, 1879.

Index

About the Author

Dr. Robert L. Scheina is a professor of History at the Industrial College of the Armed Forces, National Defense University. He is a lifelong student and author of numerous publications on the Latin American military. Within the United States, he regularly speaks at the Organization of American States' Inter-American Defense College and the U.S. Air Force Special Operations School on the past, present, and future of war in Latin America. He has also lectured at war colleges in Argentina, Canada, Chile, Ecuador, and Mexico. He holds a doctorate in Latin American history from The Catholic University of America, Washington, D.C., and a Master's Degree in Mexican history from the University of the Americas, Mexico City. He lives in the Washington, D.C., area.